Y0-DJO-664

NEW DIRECTIONS FOR STUDENT SERVICES

Margaret J. Barr, *Texas Christian University*
EDITOR-IN-CHIEF

M. Lee Upcraft, *The Pennsylvania State University*
ASSOCIATE EDITOR

Managing the Political Dimension of Student Affairs

Paul L. Moore
California State University, Chico

EDITOR

Number 55, Fall 1991

JOSSEY-BASS INC., PUBLISHERS, San Francisco
MAXWELL MACMILLAN INTERNATIONAL PUBLISHING GROUP
New York • Oxford • Singapore • Sydney • Toronto

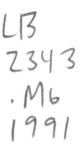

Managing the Political Dimension of Student Affairs
Paul L. Moore (ed.)
New Directions for Student Services, no. 55
Margaret J. Barr, Editor-in-Chief
M. Lee Upcraft, Associate Editor

Microfilm copies of issues and articles are available in 16mm and 35mm, as well as microfiche in 105mm, through University Microfilms Inc., 300 North Zeeb Road, Ann Arbor, Michigan 48106.

LC 85-644751   ISSN 0164-7970   ISBN 1-55542-779-0

NEW DIRECTIONS FOR STUDENT SERVICES is part of The Jossey-Bass Higher and Adult Education Series and is published quarterly by Jossey-Bass Inc., Publishers, 350 Sansome Street, San Francisco, California 94104-1310 (publication number USPS 449-070). Second-class postage paid at San Francisco, California, and at additional mailing offices. POSTMASTER: Send address changes to New Directions for Student Services, Jossey-Bass Inc., Publishers, 350 Sansome Street, San Francisco, California 94104-1310.

SUBSCRIPTIONS for 1991 cost $45.00 for individuals and $60.00 for institutions, agencies, and libraries.

EDITORIAL CORRESPONDENCE should be sent to the Editor-in-Chief, Margaret J. Barr, Sadler Hall, Texas Christian University, Fort Worth, Texas 76129.

Cover photograph by Wernher Krutein/PHOTOVAULT © 1990.

Printed on acid-free paper in the United States of America.

CONTENTS

8. Ideas for the Chief   95

Paul L. Moore

Chief student affairs officers can position themselves to respond to political
and leadership opportunities.

INDEX   105

EDITOR'S NOTES

Most of us experience and observe "politics" as we go about our jobs. The term is not unfamiliar to us and is used with some frequency across the academy. While its precise meaning may not always be clear, it does carry the connotations of "game playing," "trying to gain some advantage," "power play," and "trickery." Politics is a subject about which we feel a little uncomfortable, preferring to talk about it in the hallways or over a private lunch rather than in a staff meeting or other public setting. Nevertheless, we understand politics as a necessary and frequently positive activity through which important public decisions are made in a democratic society. Still, many of us maintain an ambivalence about using the term when describing the processes of the university.

Colleges and universities, as human institutions, do have purposes, typical structures, particular methodologies, staffs and clients, and the need to assemble and allocate resources. Whether large or small, institutions of higher education need to be managed, and an important dimension of management is decision making around issues of direction, strategy, and resource allocation. How those decisions are made is the substance of organizational politics.

The political view of organizations is certainly not the only useful perspective. Bolman and Deal (1984) have identified four major theoretical schools of thought about organizations—rational systems, human resource, political, and symbolic theories. Rational theorists are concerned with the goals, roles, and technology of organizations. Human resource theorists deal with the interaction between the needs and capabilities of people and the roles and relationships within organizations. Symbolic theorists are concerned with meaning within organizations as the point of analysis. Political theorists are concerned with power, conflict, and resource allocation. All have their strengths, weaknesses, and utility for organization managers. The political perspective can be a very useful one for university leaders.

Politics, as used in this volume, refers to the processes that produce policy and direction for an organization. Political behaviors are those behaviors designed to influence or determine institutional policy and direction. In a more formal sense, political behaviors are seen as behaviors that contribute to the maintenance or enhancement of an actor's ability to influence policy and events. Pfeffer (1981, p. 7) has given a very useful definition of organization politics: "Organizational politics involves those activities taken within organizations to acquire, develop, and use power and other resources to obtain one's preferred outcomes in a situation in which there is uncertainty or dissensus about choices." Baldridge (1971, p. 24), in his study of New York University, provides a description of the major elements of a political system, which helps to define the focus of this volume: "The broad outline of the political system looks like this: a complex social structure generates multiple pressures, many forms of power and pressure impinge on the decision makers, a legislative stage translates these pressures into policy, and a policy execution phase finally generates feedback in the form of new conflicts." Key notions are power, conflict, differing interests, influence, and decision making.

Rarely are student affairs practitioners—or university administrators in general, for that matter—formally trained in organizational behavior and the political dimension of organizational life. Instruction, when it is available, typically focuses on model behaviors or strategies from the perspectives of management, leadership, conflict resolution, organizational change, and planning. Most of us learn about institutional politics through experience, often at high personal cost, or through mentoring relationships where the mentor displays the political dimension of organizational life through action and discussion. Too frequently, student affairs administrators are caught unprepared for the sometimes bruising rough-and-tumble of institutional decision making and struggles for influence. The importance of understanding our political surroundings is stated nicely by Kaufman (1989, p. 36), speaking about university presidencies but with broader applicability: "Suffice it to say, there is a political aspect to the presidency that one overlooks at one's peril."

This volume attempts to speak openly and practically about the political dimension of managing student affairs. The authors are a uniquely experienced and knowledgeable group of professionals, from professors to presidents to line managers, all of whom have spent major portions of their careers in student affairs.

In Chapter One, James R. Appleton, a college president with extensive student affairs experience, provides the context necessary for the exploration of organizational politics. He reviews current thinking about power and its several bases, the expectations of group members and how they affect political activity, and the role of leadership in influencing political behavior.

Ronald M. Brown explores in Chapter Two the dynamics and issues that senior student affairs managers face when dealing with the president and senior members of the administration. Brown, who served many years as a vice-president at a large major public university, provides candid observations and sound advice for those working at senior managerial levels.

In Chapter Three, Paul A. Bloland, who has served as dean of students, vice-president for student affairs, and academic department chair during his long career, identifies key academic issues, values, and processes that will affect the college or university's political environment and thus the world of the chief student affairs officer.

The administrative world of the middle manager is examined in Chapter Four by two seasoned student affairs professionals, Herman Ellis and

Jim Moon. They argue that building alliances is the key to effective performance by the department head.

Daryl G. Smith, professor and former vice-president for student affairs at a small private college, writes in Chapter Five of the special issues present in small colleges and religious institutions. She identifies the distinctive characteristics of these institutions and their special challenges for student affairs officers.

In Chapter Six, Helen L. Mamarchev and Mary Lynn Williamson, experienced administrators in a major public university, identify, through interviews with women and minority professionals, the issues and concerns of women and minorities who are operating in the political environment of student affairs.

In Chapter Seven, M. Lee Upcraft, an experienced administrator and faculty member, and his colleague, Thomas G. Poole, a student affairs administrator and ethicist, write about the dilemmas of managing in an ethical way in the sometimes messy real world, and they provide a model to help professionals think and act in an ethical manner when confronted with political challenges.

Chapter Eight details practical strategies and advice for chief student affairs officers. The advice is drawn from the earlier chapters, the literature, and the author's experience.

This volume is intended to stimulate thought among student affairs and university administrators about the nature and potential of the political environment in which we all participate and to provide practical guidance to the practitioner. It will also, I hope, encourage more academic attention to this important perspective on college and university management and leadership.

I would like to express my deep appreciation for the willing and easy collaboration of the authors, many of whom have been mentors and colleagues over many years. Their competence makes a task like this a pleasure. Special thanks are also gratefully given to Patricia Hoiland, who managed the transcript-development process with such precision and enthusiasm.

Paul L. Moore
Editor

References

Baldridge, V. J. *Power and Conflict in the University.* New York: Wiley, 1971.
Bolman, L. G., and Deal, T. E. *Modern Approaches to Understanding and Managing Organizations.* San Francisco: Jossey-Bass, 1984.
Kaufman, J. F. "Strategies for an Effective Presidency." In *On Assuming a College or University Presidency: Lessons and Advice from the Field.* Washington, D.C.: American Association for Higher Education, 1989.
Pfeffer, J. *Power in Organizations.* Marshfield, Mass.: Pitman Publishing, 1981.

Paul L. Moore is vice-president for student affairs at California State University, Chico.

The leader's ability to influence policy and events and take advantage of the expectations and performance of others will be enhanced by an understanding of political behavior within organizations.

The Context

James R. Appleton

Most student affairs professionals, when asked to define the organization for which they have some responsibility, tend to think first about the specific purpose or function(s) of the college or university, or the specific programs and services for which they are responsible. Or the bureaucratic realities of the organization come to mind—such variables as size, structure, hierarchies within the institution, budgets, information flow, and control. Yet, as Moore has stated in the Editor's Notes, each of our colleges and universities is also a political organization. There exists a dynamic, a continual tug, an ongoing attempt by the persons who identify with the college or a given division, such as student affairs, to enhance their own ability to influence policy and events. Political behavior is inevitable in every organizational setting, is found at every level in the hierarchy, and intensifies as the decision possibilities are greater and more important.

Colleges and universities are especially susceptible to political behavior because they are goal-diffuse and affected by an unusually complex set of constituencies and organizational patterns. It is more difficult to define teaching and learning than the manufacturing of a specific product. Indeed, is teaching the primary purpose, or do research and scholarly activity or community service take precedence?

Moreover, the means as well as the goals are not as precise as might be desired and are easily influenced by the variety of constituencies and self-serving interests within the college or university. No organization exists that is not encumbered by competing demands, but few exceed the complexity brought about by the sometimes conflicting interests of faculty, students, alumni, parents, community members, donors, and governmental agencies. The hierarchical structures themselves are probably unique. While

the members of a governing board maintain fiduciary and legal responsibility and assume that the president and administrative team that they hire
will manage the campus, a broad range of both policy and procedural
authority is delegated to faculty, and students clamor for the ability to
govern their own lives. Faculty, not to be considered typical corporate
employees, are pulled among loyalties to the college, their areas of scholar-
ship and professional interest, and the profession itself.

To complicate the picture even further, the impact of this never-ending
struggle for influence may be exaggerated in its importance. In response to
the question of why there is so much political activity at the college, one
wag readily responded with a rephrasing of a familiar line: "Because the
stakes are so low."

It is our objective not only to understand something about political
behavior within colleges and universities, and specifically student affairs,
but also to enhance the leader's ability to influence policy and events. To
this end, this chapter is organized around several emphases, as follows: (1)
a presentation of the kinds and bases of power available within organizations (with references to colleges and universities and student affairs); (2)
special attention to how the expectations of the members of the organization influence our thinking about political behavior and how to take advantage of this reality; and (3) the importance of the leader's having a vision
of what is to be accomplished in order to bring about the desired congruence between individual members' expectations and performance and institutional objectives.

The Power to Act Politically

To understand, hold, and wisely use power is essential to effective leadership in any organization. Colleges and universities, and such units as student affairs, are not exempt. The acquisition and right use of power is part
of the dynamic process of affecting change or meeting institutional objectives and personal ambitions. It is part of the currency of the organization,
with everyone not necessarily heading in the same direction. Conflict is normal, and clout must be built to complete the tasks at hand.

Kinds and Bases of Power. *Power,* for our purposes, is defined as "the
basic energy to initiate and sustain action or, to put it another way, the
capacity to translate intention into reality and sustain it" (Bennis and
Nanus, 1985, p. 17). There are several kinds or bases of power, which have
been described in a number of ways by various authors. The following
formulation, drawn heavily from Webber (1985), Gannon (1982), Appleton,
Briggs, and Rhatigan (1978), French and Raven (1959), Baldridge (1971),
and Baldridge, Curtis, Ecker, and Riley (1978), may be helpful.

Bureaucratic Power. Gannon (1982, p. 352) calls this "legitimate power";
Appleton, Briggs, and Rhatigan, (1978, p. 56) refer to "authority given." It is
"the core of a traditional influence system, in which leadership positions

are endowed with formal authority" (Webber, 1985, p. 187). Bureaucratic power is based on the idea that the person with this formal authority has the ability to allocate resources and to reward, employ, promote, and release employees. It also often involves access to authority and control of information flow. The degree to which a given person possesses bureaucratic power is a function of the size of budgets, the breadth of the administrative portfolio, the number of persons supervised, the information accessed, and, often, the position enjoyed by the person within the administrative hierarchy (Gannon, 1982, p. 13).

Professional Resource Power. Termed *referent power* by many writers, professional resource power may be described as the influence that accrues to relationships with important constituencies and benefits from the follower's desire to identify with the leader who seems important. Examples might involve an attorney who benefits from the prestige of a bar association, or the influence of the American Medical Association in relation to the impact of the comparable organization for social workers. For the professional serving in a staff position, reference depends in part on the level in the organization and the recognized power of the supervisor.

Coercion. Webber (1985, p. 187) states that "coercive power is based on a follower's perception that the influencer has the ability to punish and that the punishment will be unpleasant and frustrating." The use of force is a legitimate but somewhat questionable power, available in every organization. Quite important as a tool for labor unions, it is also available to student and community groups—through, for instance, a threat of bad publicity or an appeal to public opinion.

Personal-Influence Power. There are a number of ways to extend one's influence that can be grouped under this heading—for example, building coalitions around a particular interest or issue, or developing informal relationships within an organization, relationships that can be called on when support is required. Accomplishments that are only tangential to the mission can increase one's credibility, such as publications or serving on accreditation teams. Interestingly enough, myths that develop about one's past or reputation will also increase the influence that comes through personal charisma and stature.

Expert Power. A most important base of power, a subset of personal-influence power that is easily overlooked, is the power that can be realized through the exercise of sheer competence and through the belief that the leader has special knowledge or expertise. This has to do, in part, with the leader's being able to achieve what has been promised (Appleton, Briggs, and Rhatigan, 1978). This leads to influence won through respect, not assertion.

Application to Student Affairs

Let us reflect for a moment on the realities of power for the student affairs administrator. If the objective is to think politically in an attempt to influence policy and events, then what kinds of power are available? Certainly, there are aspects of bureaucratic power that one would automatically identify, and this is what brings many student affairs administrators to a defensive posture. By comparison with the academic vice-president or the chief financial officer, the student affairs administrator does not usually have a wide range of responsibility, budget centers, and numbers of personnel. The use of these bureaucratic resources to exert influence should not be minimized, but the relative starting points that accrue to various administrative units need to be recognized.

The student affairs administrator should also be aware of the modest referent power that is typically available. The National Association of Student Personnel Administrators, or comparable professional organizations structured appropriately to provide service and assistance to the active professional, do not carry the clout of the American Medical Association, for example. Except for the clinicians in our midst, or maybe the financial aid officers, there is not a body of knowledge easily recognized by the community within higher education as a basis of professional activity in student affairs. "Anyone can be a dean, with a bit of common sense and a little experience" is a common perspective. Visualize, for a moment, a governing-board meeting in which both a modification in the medical school's curriculum and some policy change in student life appear on the agenda. It is likely that the members of the board will depend on the professional wisdom of the medical school's dean and promptly approve a change in the curriculum. The conversation about the policy change in student affairs is likely to be lengthy, with many of those present acting as if they have some corner on the truth, and with the dean's professional opinion being viewed as less influential. This is not to imply that the student affairs professional is devoid of referent power, but it is limited.

Some years ago, a student affairs vice-president was accorded the honor of being named by *Change* magazine as one of the emerging young leaders in the academy. For months following this event, deans, faculty, alumni, and even students seemed to listen and respond more quickly. While the confidence of the vice-president may also have been buoyed a bit by the recognition, this serves as a ready example of the influence of referent power.

The student affairs professional has access to a group with which coalitions can be built and with whom coercion can be exercised to accomplish important ends—the students. This, however, would be a serious misuse of power and would complicate the role and responsibility of the administrative staff. Moreover, use of coercion is often an admission of failure in the minds of student affairs administrators, and in many settings the threat can be used only once. In the extreme, consider the valued administrator who threatens, for example, to leave the institution unless some requested change is made in personal working conditions or policy.

The threat may succeed on a given occasion. The second time around, the threat may be accepted. The adage "Be careful what you ask for because you may get it" comes to mind.

The advantage that personal influence brings is too often underplayed, and the power that derives from being capable is given less credit than is deserved. Indeed, sheer competence is not only important in its own right but can also serve as a counterbalance to the bureaucracy. At least these questions should be considered: Should the student affairs leader strive for more bureaucratic power? Should more attention be paid to alternate bases of power, to influence policy and programs and meet understood objectives?

The responses are obvious and lead to a sampling of suggestions that encourage the student affairs administrator to take advantage of the several bases of power within the college or university, in order to manage the political dimensions of student affairs more effectively:

1. Determine who has the power, and what kind.
2. Recognize differences among individual needs and expectations, and decide which of them can be met. (This will be considered in more detail in this chapter.)
3. Decide which aspects of bureaucratic power are more accessible, and develop strategies. For example, develop information networks to access information. Accept responsiblity for new programs. Develop budgetary plans that reduce costs in one area to improve an area of greater importance. Be alert to organizational changes.
4. Build coalitions by discovering persons or groups to support, promote, and help in sustaining the idea, program, or policy change that is desired.
5. Determine ways to increase individual competence by engaging in training and continuing education, volunteering for additional responsibility for individual and organizational gain, learning to anticipate issues or ways to improve the program before being asked, seeking feedback, conceptualizing how to handle the stress and decisions of the person a step ahead in the hierarchy, or learning how to function as effectively in project management as in the tasks of line responsibility.
6. Do not fight over an issue unless there is some possibility of winning. Never fight without a goal in mind, and be selective in choosing where to influence and for what purpose. Emphasize the most important thing, thereby concentrating your efforts.

How Expectations of Organization Members Help Define Political Activity

In addition to recognizing the bases of available power, it is important to pay attention to how the expectations of organization members influence the understanding of political behavior. When it comes to focusing on the political behavior of individual members of the college or university, Baldridge (1971) is helpful in defining *political activity* as any behavior of organization members that meets the special interests of individuals or groups. Such activity is self-serving and can be thought of as acting in such a manner as to achieve personal objectives or acquire and use power and authority to achieve personal objectives in an organization.

At first blush, this seems devious or inappropriate. This is where the notion of playing politics, with its negative connotations, is derived. Indeed, acting to achieve personal objectives within an organization may not help others or the organization itself in achieving what are the most important objectives. By this time, however, the proposition ought to be clear that this is not necessarily so. Political behavior is not necessarily bad, does not necessarily involve trickery or deception, is not always negative, and is not necessarily dysfunctional to the best interests of the organization. Whether the acquisition and use of power and authority on the part of individuals to achieve personal objectives is functional or dysfunctional will depend on a recognition of the various reasons why persons join and continue in organizations and on an understanding of the ability of members and leaders to bring about congruence between individual intent and organizational desires.

Individual Motives or Reasons for Being Part of the Organization. Members type, write, operate machines, raise funds, serve on committees, teach, do research, counsel, organize and plan programs, and manage services. This list represents the work of members on behalf of their organizations, almost always accomplished by the interaction of members with one another. Their performance varies in relation to their skills, the resources available that enable them to function, the various roles assigned or available, their positions in the hierarchy, and their expectations and motives.

Organization members bring certain expectations to the organization, which may be influenced by personal values, goals, beliefs, gender, ethnicity, previous training, or experience. It is clear that these expectations do have an impact on performance—that is, there is an interdependence between expectation and performance. By *expectation*, we mean what members anticipate in becoming a part of the organization and what they expect to gain. Why are they there, and why do they stay? What is their estimated value of the organization itself? What are their self-serving reasons for being in the organization?

It would be an interesting exercise for readers to derive such lists by analyzing their own reasons and those of close colleagues. Why are you in the position you hold in the organization in which you work? A partial list assembled from discussion with a number of employees might include the following elements:

- To earn enough money to survive
- To become wealthy or to earn enough to live comfortably
- Belief in the institution's mission, wanting to do good things
- Satisfaction gained from performing to the best of one's ability
- Professional growth
- Possibility of mobility within a profession or the organization itself
- Security
- Status or prestige of position
- Status or prestige of the organization
- Working conditions, atmosphere, or associates
- Location
- Personal recognition received.

Notice that the reasons range from mere survival to ideas that carry with them a good deal of altruism and lofty ambition. Wage or salary expectations have been separated into two levels. Each member of the organization will have one or more (usually several) of these reasons or expectations in mind. Many can even rank these or other reasons, if prompted to be thoughtful about such matters. Admittedly, some of the reasons are in conflict with others; clarity and consistency in responses are often difficult. Moreover, different individuals in the same organization are likely to have widely divergent reasons or expectations. There is nothing intrinsically wrong with any of these expectations or self-serving motives.

It is very important to recognize that how expectations are ranked also influences behavior—political behavior, if you will. If two individuals in the same organization have very different sets of expectations, this is important to know. If conflicting expectations are embodied in a given person, this may begin to enable some understanding about the behavior of this employee.

Self-Serving Behavior: Functional or Dysfunctional? Irrespective of the assignment of tasks or the organization's reason for employing an individual or using a volunteer, the individual has myriad and sometimes complex reasons for joining and continuing with the organization. A logical next question arises: How can one distinguish between political activity that can support institutional objectives (or at least be neutral) and those behaviors that are dysfunctional or negatively affect goal attainment? The answer is simply by determining to what degree the individual's expectations are congruent with, or at least neutral to, the objectives of the organization. This statement may be understood with reference to Figure 1. The organization in which the overlap between A and B is larger is probably the more successful organization.

This illustration starts to make clear why some persons may or may not support obviously good proposals, or why some employees are motivated differently from how others are. (For student affairs personnel, it is

Figure 1. Goal: Functional Behavior

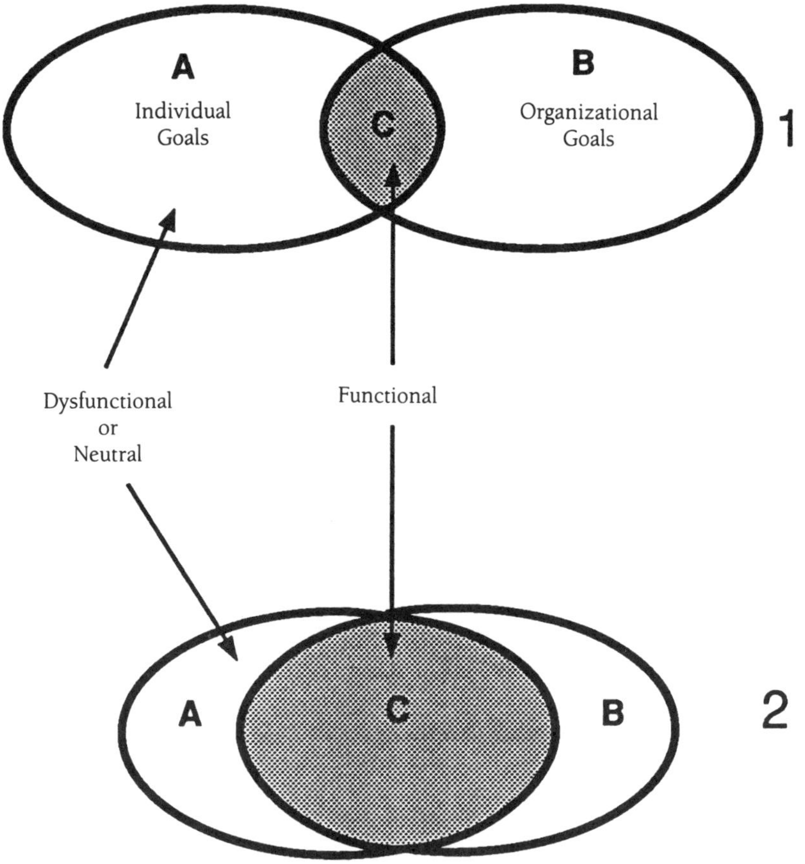

useful to point out that these same analyses can be adapted to the question of why students come to and remain at a given institution.) It may help us understand why some persons behave in certain ways at meetings or in individual discussions, and why one person will work to enhance the success of others while another seems to enjoy embarrassing a colleague. Most important, it helps us recognize something more about the political behavior of organizations.

Responsibility of the Leader

Effective leaders are the persons who are most successful in influencing the activities of members in efforts toward goal achievement on behalf of the organization. Leaders adapt what they do and how they do it to their own unique strengths, expectations, and styles, to what makes the employees and others in the organization tick, and to the particular tasks and nature of the organization itself. Notice how much leadership activity is affected by this discussion of political behavior. In fact, a discussion of political behavior and power is a necessary precursor to a discussion of leadership performance, activity, and individual style.

We recognize that organizations are defined not only by purpose and in bureaucratic terms but also as political entities. We have considered the importance of power in enabling us to define political behavior, and we understand that organization members sometimes embody complex and often conflicting sets of expectations. What is the role of the leader? How can we help motivate those for whom we bear some degree of responsibility into performing effectively on behalf of the organization? How can we manage the political dimension of our institutions?

The answer may be self-evident: the leader must be prepared to use power in an effective manner and to understand the extent to which individual differences and expectations and self-serving political interests will affect the functioning of an organization. The leader must also have a clear sense of the mission and objectives, as well as of how much individual differences and expectations affect the performance of employees. The leader can then provide opportunities, organize tasks, and direct individuals in such a way that they can satisfy their needs and expectations as much as possible while also striving to accomplish the objectives of the organization.

This suggests that we must not deny the expectations of various individuals—indeed, that we must respect, understand, value, moderate as appropriate, and use individual expectations and motives to satisfy institutional objectives. On occasion, this may also call for modifying, over time, the objectives of the organization or the means of accomplishing the objectives.

As leaders of personnel and programs, our job is, to a large extent, to ensure as much congruence as possible between these individuals and the organizational objectives and desires and to bring personal behavior, as affected by performance and expectations, into as functional a relation as possible with the organizational objectives.

The leader is charged to take into account the unique features of the other person, the richness that a given employee brings by virtue of gender or ethnicity, the realities that age and experience bring to expectations, and the alternating needs for security and mobility that are sometimes embodied even in one individual. Does the person respond better to a participatory style of management or to a more directed style, and why? Does criticism or encouragement prompt a more useful response? Does encouraging people to use their own judgment or engaging them in an outline of alternatives produce the best result? How can the organization be structured to platform the most skilled and interested persons?

A more detailed example may be helpful. A supervisor may discover that a member of the staff is working on an advanced degree in planning. This person is the budget officer of the unit, and an excellent employee. The supervisor begins to discover that one of the key reasons why this employee stays in her job is not that the largest possible salary is available in this position but that the job meshes well with her graduate studies and her interest in upward mobility. Doing more for the organization, as time is available, will provide relevant career experience and enhance her career mobility. The supervisor has no additional salary to offer but notes that this is not the primary motivation, after all. The supervisor continues to load the job with more responsibilites, especially in planning and forecasting. With more responsibility comes enthusiasm because the job contributes both to the value of the organization and to the employee's interests. Other employees, more interested in security or wages as a primary motivator, may react to such job loading in a very different fashion.

One further consideration about the leader may be relevant here: more than anything else, successful leaders marshal the skills of others by the sheer weight of their vision. In the context of this dialogue, presidents must have vision about how to influence their organizations through the right use of power and about how to take account of individual members' expectations in light of the objectives that are important to the organization.

Bennis and Nanus (1985, p. 25) note that leaders are a widely diverse group. They are "right-brained and left-brained, tall and short, fat and thin, articulate and inarticulate, assertive and retiring, dressed for success and dressed for failure, participative and autocratic." They might also have said that they are young and old, black and white, men and women with skills and characteristics that vary significantly. What is similar? What is the marrow of successful leadership behavior? Four variables are noted, three of which are left to your own reading of this useful text; the other and most important is that those who are successful in leading others marshal the skills of others through the sheer weight of vision.

The successful leaders interviewed "had an agenda, an unparalleled concern with the outcome. Leaders are the most results-oriented individuals" (Bennis and Nanus, 1985, p. 28). While certain skills must be mastered, the vision is compelling and pulls people toward the leader. The vision creates focus. "Intensity coupled with commitment is magnetic. . . . Vision grabs. Initially it grabs the leader and enables others also to get on the bandwagon" (Bennis and Nanus, 1985, p. 28). Leaders are shapers, not reactors.

Understanding the political realities of the college and university as well as the objectives of the organization, recognizing the interaction of expectations and performance on the part of the members of the institution, and learning to appropriately use the power available to bring these variables into some congruence with institutional objectives will provide the grist for the development of the agenda, the vision, of the successful leader in student affairs.

References

Appleton, J. R., Briggs, C. M., and Rhatigan, J. J. *Pieces of Eight*. Portland, Ore.: NASPA Institute of Research and Development, 1978.

Baldridge, J. V. *Power and Conflict in the University*. New York: Wiley, 1971.

Baldridge, J. V., Curtis, D. Y., Ecker, G., and Riley, G. L. *Policy Making and Effective Leadership*. San Francisco: Jossey-Bass, 1978.

Bennis, W., and Nanus, B. *Leaders: The Strategies for Taking Charge*. New York: Harper & Row, 1985.

French, J.R.P., and Raven, B. H. "The Bases of Social Power." In D. Cartwright (ed.), *Studies in Social Power*. Ann Arbor: University of Michigan Press, 1959.

Gannon, M. J. *Management and Integrated Framework*. (2nd ed.) Boston: Little, Brown, 1982.

Webber, R. A. *Management*. (3rd ed.) Homewood, Ill.: Irwin, 1985.

James R. Appleton is president and university professor at University of Redlands, California.

The chief student affairs officer must be a leader, but being an effective staff officer and colleague is equally important.

Working with the President and Senior Administrators

Ronald M. Brown

Other chapters in this book are intended to help you become a better leader as chief student affairs officer. Leadership is an extremely important part of your role, and to the directors, counselors, program coordinators, and dishwashers who work in your part of your university, you are a leader.

This chapter, however, will give you some suggestions on being a better follower and supporter as you work with your president and will address some ways to be a more effective colleague as you work with your peers. In some respects, your roles as follower and colleague are more important than that of leader, since you will fail as a leader if you are not in tune with the other executive officers and senior administrative staff, your president (or chancellor, or whoever is your boss), and the board that appointed him or her.

To help you be a better chief student affairs officer, and thus to help your president and administrative team to mold a more effective learning environment for your students, this chapter will discuss the importance of what you do both to enhance and to create the learning environment, the varied roles a vice-president must play, your relationship with your president, and some ways to work better with your peers and colleagues. The discussion will be about vice-presidents and presidents, but the principles are the same, regardless of whether you are a vice-chancellor reporting to a chancellor, an associate provost reporting to a provost, a dean of students reporting to a vice-president, or whatever titles and responsibilities you, your supervisor, and your peers may carry.

New Directions for Student Services, no. 55, Fall 1991 © Jossey-Bass Inc., Publishers

Hold Your Head High

Psychologists and theologians teach that we must understand and accept ourselves before we can do the same for others. So it is with being a follower and a colleague: we must know who we are and what we are about before we can deal effectively with our superiors and peers. During more than three decades in university student affairs administration, I have attended several hundred conferences, committee meetings, and workshops involving thousands of professionals in the field. I can report that informal conversations at such conclaves take about ten minutes to turn to the theme song of the profession: "Why Don't They Love Me?" Formal conference sessions take a little longer to raise the same question.

There are many verses to the song, but the prevailing leitmotif is that student affairs administrators consider themselves to be second-class citizens on their campuses. Please note the reflexive use of the verb: they look on themselves as second-class citizens.

In my years as vice-president for student affairs, there undoubtedly were some faculty members, academic affairs administrators, business officers, and quite a few students and parents whose evaluations would have required me to move up several notches to achieve second class. There are countless instances where I felt the same about them, but I never thought of myself or of my work as second class.

Nobody else is going to think of you as first class unless you look on yourself as a person of competence doing a job that is essential to the organizational health of the institution; to the well-being of students, who happen also to be children learning to be adults, with all the needs and shortcomings that go with that condition; and, above all, to that mysterious process called learning. At the risk of my repeating the primary message of every sales manual, I urge you to think positively. You must think well of yourself and of your profession before you can expect others to do the same.

The Importance of What You Do. Too often, I think, we who work in the student affairs area consider what we do to be of a lesser significance than other university activities. Although some universities have research and public service as part of their function in society, the primary role of every university is helping students learn. Teaching is central to that process, and faculty members are important because of that centrality, but it is not the only way students learn.

Aiding and Abetting Learning. The librarian has to have the books and other learning resources available. The computer technician has to have the hardware and software up and running. The chief student affairs officer has to make sure that students have financing, housing, food, recreation, and all the other necessities and support systems that must be available if effective learning is to take place.

Let us suppose that an eminent surgeon has just completed a successful heart transplant. Then let us suppose that the patient is in postoperative intensive care and the nurse spots a dramatic drop in blood pressure and expertly moves to stabilize and then restore it to normal. Who has saved the patient's life?

Now let us suppose that Joe Merit Scholar is sitting in a classroom and facing a professor who is renowned for original research of great importance to humanity and who has published fourteen books acclaimed by scholars for their accuracy and by the laity because of their exquisite clarity. The great Professor Schnarf, *mirabile dictu,* also delivers lectures that elicit standing ovations, is readily accessible for office consultations, and gives wise counsel at frequent fireside chats. But Joe has not learned anything for the last month because his parents are getting a divorce, his girl friend has ridden off on the rear seat of a motorcycle, and he has lost his last hundred dollars in a fraternity poker game. Let us now suppose that Joe turns to the counseling center, gets help in dealing with his personal problems, is referred for an emergency loan, and is able to get back on the academic track. Who has saved Joe's education and his future?

Ten Thousand Classrooms. We who work in the student personnel area are not responsible only for support systems. We also are responsible for creating, abetting, and enhancing another curriculum outside the classrooms, laboratories, and libraries. All too often, this role is overlooked or thought to be of no consequence.

In part, I am thinking of the formal programming done by student unions, deans of students, counseling centers, residence halls, and others. But I am thinking also of the white student who learns something about being human when randomly assigned a black roommate, of the significant learning that takes place when a freshman learns he is out of money by November because of the huge stack of CD's he bought in early September, and of the young woman who stuck it out in spite of receiving no sorority bid and realized that she could function quite well even though her mother still cries through every telephone call home. That is where learning takes place, and that is where we come in. We, too, are teachers, and we teach all over the campus and far beyond, in thousands of ways seen and unseen.

Learning by Friction. On my campus, we generally have about six hundred registered student organizations. Some are composed of three people concerned about an issue of the moment, and the group lasts ten days. Others have large memberships and have been related to the campus for many decades. Some fulfill the highest ambitions of service, some seem only to worship the Great God Alcohol, and some just want to raise hell.

The only tangible benefits that any of these organizations receive by registering are a degree of legitimacy and the right to use university facilities for meetings, rallies, or demonstrations. One of those facilities is the West Mall, a broad, tree-shaded pedestrian thoroughfare traversed by thousands of students, faculty, and staff. Registered organizations may reserve a table from which they peddle their intellectual wares, and each weekday sees twenty or thirty tables set up. They are pro-Israel and pro-PLO, prochoice and prolife, Young Democrats and Young Libertarians, sailing enthusiasts and fencers. They represent every possible viewpoint, every sect and tribal affiliation. Whether or not you have read Hegel, you are instantly aware that ideas are being rubbed against other ideas, young minds are moving from thesis to antithesis to synthesis and back again, and learning is taking place at a furious rate.

It takes two full-time professional members of the dean of students' staff, backed up by support staff and additional professionals when needed, to work with these organizations and to monitor the West Mall. A campus policeman is on hand through the noon hour because enthusiasm sometimes gets out of hand. You cannot tell me that those staff members are not helping students learn.

What Is a Vice-President?

As chief student affairs officer, you have many roles to play and myriad expectations placed on you. Sometimes these are in accord with one another, and sometimes they clash, with you in the middle. Here are some of the tasks you are called upon to perform.

Surrogate. Having established to your own satisfaction that you are competent and that the work you do is important, you need to understand the importance of the role of vice-president (or of whatever other second-tier administrative position you occupy).

Contrary to the view held by some, a vice-president is not a mouse learning how to become a rat. The adjective in the title comes from the Latin *vicis,* meaning "exchange," "alternation," or "stead." It implies that the holder acts as an extension of the president and is considerably more than just another staff member giving advice. I am well aware that not every relationship between president and vice-president works that way, but that is the goal. As chief student affairs officer, you need to be able to speak on behalf of your president, with at least 90 percent confidence that you are accurately reflecting his or her personal views, as well as the institution's position on the subject.

Shield and Defender. Speaking on behalf of or instead of the president is a significant role because the president cannot be everywhere when needed. There is another reason for the surrogate role, however.

At one point in my career, I served under a president whose background was in labor-management relations. He was an excellent negotiator, but in dealings with student groups making demands of the sort so common in the 1960s, the fact that he was chairing the negotiations left him and us with no place to go. We could not say, "That sounds like a fairly good idea, but I'll have to get together with the president and get back to you." We had no way to caucus, to take the temperature of the governing board, or simply to sleep on it, because the Big Man was right there in the room. Students, like most other people outside the administrative circle, view the president as having virtually unfettered power and expect an immediate answer. They do not understand that a president is more like Gulliver, tied to the ground by a thousand tiny threads.

Thus, when I became a vice-president, my new president made it clear that part of my task was to play field commander and take some of the fire so that, in the best long-range interests of the institution, he could stay back in headquarters and direct the battle on all its fronts and with greater breadth of view. Not all presidents understand this principle, and many vice-presidents do not want to work that way, even if they understand it, but the vice-president's front-line role is essential to an effective working relationship and to the overall effectiveness of the administrative team. The goal is not so much to protect the president as to shelter the presidency and thereby the institution.

How to Train a President

What if you understand this kind of relationship, perhaps even have enjoyed such circumstances in earlier times, but your president wants to be immersed in the action and speaks out on issues or makes commitments without having all the necessary information? How do you keep your president informed, knowledgeable, and committed regarding student affairs and students services?

This chapter began with the assertion that a vice-president is a follower as well as a leader. Many would see this strictly as the vice-president's taking directives from the president and executing them, but any good educator knows that the best followers teach as much as they learn. You must teach your president at every turn, but what should you teach?

Knowing the Territory. Assuming that you have it clear in your own mind that what you do is important, a very significant part of your communication is to do your best to make sure that your president sees some of the light you have found.

For openers, you must tend to such seemingly simple things as making sure your president knows what administrative units are in your purview. He or she must become acquainted with the director or dean of each. This does not happen automatically unless a disaster befalls one of the units, such as publicity about nude sunbathing in the courtyard of a residence hall. You must work hard at making it happen by giving presidential tours, asking a director to join you when discussing an issue in his or her area with the president, or creating opportunities for your staff to meet the president socially.

Sharing Values. Having familiarized the president with what you do and who makes it happen, the more difficult and important task is to communicate why you do it—the philosophical foundation discussed earlier. Although you can try to do this by writing memoranda or by booking time for a formal presentation, with visuals and all the devices at your disposal, I am convinced that values are communicated over the long term, one event and one issue at a time. For instance, you can communicate values when you discuss how to handle a case of academic dishonesty involving a major donor's daughter, when you defend the counseling center's budget, when you wrestle with the problems of recruiting and graduating more minority students, and when you strive to preserve the right of speakers to be heard even when their ideas are outrageous. These daily events and decisions form the crucible in which your values and those of your president and colleagues are forged and shared.

The Matter of Advocacy. As you work through these and myriad other issues involving students, a large part of your role is to act as advocate for students, their welfare, and their rights. Indeed, most students, especially student leaders, see this as your only role. They are wrong: you have a responsibility for the welfare of the institution over time, across boxes on the organizational chart, and into the broader social environment outside your ivied walls.

You are, in fact, in a boundary role, communicating students' concerns and needs to your president and others and at the same time helping students see some of the broader picture. Using an example just cited, you may find yourself fighting to invite to campus a radical speaker chosen by a student committee and then imposing disciplinary action on students who heckle and disrupt the speech. The two roles are difficult to balance because they involve ambiguity, the breeding ground of conflict.

I know of no administrative job of any consequence that does not involve considerable ambiguity. If there is a clear and correct solution to a problem, it likely will be handled through routine policy or by support staff. When an issue reaches the president or a vice-president, it is there because there are equally desirable claims on limited funds, time, or space or, too often, because there are equally bad outcomes.

You are an advocate for students, but you always must temper advocacy with judgment and vision. You are an advocate for the institution, but you must temper your assurance of institutional rightness with awareness that the students may just turn out to be right.

The Filter System. With so much information constantly being loaded into the presidential memory, your task is to decide when you should share a problem with your president and when you should not bother him or her. You can try to let your president know everything you know, but then what are you doing in office?

Your president has to know about new developments in molecular biology, current laws regarding intellectual property and unrelated business income, the mood of a prominent faculty member holding an offer from

Fatcat University, the board member who is about to attack, and what food is to be served at the annual dinner for big donors. That is only between 8:00 and 9:00 A.M. on Monday, with more to come, and not counting any of the land mines you have spotted in student affairs.

There are no easy rules on when to tell your president of a problem, but, subjective and contextual though this list may be, I can give you some examples. I called, met with, or sent a quick note to my presidents when:

The financial aid director left town hurriedly with his girl friend, the family cat, and several thousand dollars of our money.

A student was found dead of alcohol poisoning in a setting that suggested a fraternity relationship.

We were about to cast a minority vote (something like 500-3, as I recall) on a highly publicized NCAA issue presumably involving virtue.

A potentially difficult rally or demonstration was planned.

An unexpected question was likely to be asked at a meeting with students ("Dr. Smith, why don't you do something about the grackles outside my dorm room?").

The band proposed new uniforms in burnt orange instead of the liturgically correct bright orange.

An event or comment was likely to generate negative publicity in the news media or unfavorable reactions among the board (or unexpected good news came along, so that the president could take credit for it).

Presidents do not like and do not deserve unpleasant surprises. Painful as it is to be the one calling with bad news, it is far better that it be you than a newspaper reporter or a board member who calls at two in the morning. The nearest I can come to a rule on getting news to your president is "When in doubt, do." When either you or your president is new in the job, you must especially err on the side of providing more information rather than less.

This rule applies to long-term issues and institutional folkways, as well as to fast-breaking news. You may know that it is an affront to human decency and a threat to survival of your university if the president does not attend the Big Game, but the new president may not be aware of this, and you must be sure that a trip to Ulan Bator does not get scheduled for that weekend.

The Emperor's Clothes. Perhaps the most difficult task for any administrative officer at any level is to disagree with one's superior. After all, your boss ultimately controls how much you are paid, your working conditions, and even whether you continue to have a job. Few of us, including presidents, like disagreement, yet how can your president act knowledgeably and avoid being blindsided if you do not share your views openly? As Bennis (1989) comments, silence, not dissent, is the one answer a leader should not accept. You owe it to your president, your institution, and your own integrity to voice your dissent, and your president has an obligation to listen.

The Limits of Loyalty. Early in my service as vice-president for student affairs, I was asked what I would do if the president took an action with which I disagreed strongly. My response was as follows: I have a responsibility to make my views privately known to my president and my colleagues, and I must listen to their rebuttals. Then, if I disagree with the outcome, I have three choices. I can walk out of the room and support the decision, I can walk out and say nothing, or I can resign. Unfortunately, it is much easier to rationalize the first two options than the third, but every administrator has to have a line that cannot be breached. One important note about resignation: you can threaten to resign only once, because the next time your offer will be viewed as just that—a threat—and it almost certainly will be accepted.

In the same vein, there is a school of thought that calls for vice-presidents to submit pro forma resignations upon appointment of a new president, much like a Hindu widow's throwing her body on her husband's funeral pyre. If the new president asks for mass resignations or even just for yours, you must accede and resign graciously, for you always serve at the pleasure of your president. Never initiate the action, however. I know of one case where such a resignation was submitted by a vice-president who actually wanted to remain. The president did not know it was just a formality, accepted it with true regret, and realized the misunderstanding only after the replacement had been appointed.

You and Your Peers

Most of this discussion has been about working with your president, and rightly so, because he or she is your leader. But your relationships with the other vice-presidents can be of equal or greater importance in determining your success. What are some things to know about working with them?

The Organizational Chart. The most that can be said about tables of organization, with their boxes and lines, is that they tell you how an institution is supposed to work. With all due deference to Max Weber and to most books on management, rarely is that the case. Why?

The Underfilled Box. The first answer is that some of your peers are not competent or are too lazy to fill their boxes. Whatever their job descriptions, they do not fulfill them. Perhaps they never were very good, or they simply may have worn out. Perhaps they were appointed to please a long-dead member of your board or have been around so long they have de facto tenure. Others may be competent and ambitious but not in tune with the current administrative leadership. Why does the president not dismiss them? As you surely know from managing your own staff, firing someone takes a huge amount of emotional energy, especially if you dislike grievance hearings, depositions, television interviews detailing an illustrious career, and letters from alumni who remember Dean Snafu as he was in the old days. Whatever the reason, the work does not get done where it is supposed to be done, leaving a vacuum.

The Overfilled Box. How is the vacuum filled? It is filled by someone else, of course—sometimes by one of the weak vice-president's subordinates, but often by one of the other vice-presidents, who may be ambitious and eager to acquire more territory or just may be dedicated and committed. Again, the chart fails to tell you the true story and is actually misleading.

Tangled Lines. The lines on the organizational table can be just as erroneous as the box labels. They may show all vice-presidents reporting directly to the president, when the fact is that some of them function fairly independently while others have much more influence on and contact with the president than their supposed peers do. Some may see the president only at commencement.

Townsend (1970) says that a dotted line on an organizational chart means trouble. He is correct: it means ambiguity, and, as I have said, ambiguity leads to misunderstanding and conflict. To Townsend's rule I would add another: if a title includes the word *special,* it usually also means trouble, and for the same reason.

The Phantoms. There is another group of people who do not appear on the chart at all but who hold enormous power because of longevity, intelligence, and drive. I have always worked very hard to earn and deserve the trust of the executive assistants, administrative associates, and assistants who accomplish so much and yet almost never make a speech, sit on a platform, or attend a banquet. They are the power plants who make the vehicle run while the president and vice-presidents do the steering or, sometimes, pretend to do the steering. My efforts to develop trust with support staff were not calculated or devious. So far as I know, I never abused that trust. But having the support of those people has been very important to me.

Off the Chart. The point of all this discussion about underfilled and overfilled boxes, lines, and phantoms is that your success as chief student affairs officer may well hinge on how well you understand the way things really work, instead of on your stumbling along as if they worked the way they ought to. Obviously, this is most important if you are a total newcomer, but the cast of characters is always changing, and you must remain current even if you are the kid who has been on the block the longest.

The Positive Value of Gossip. Textbooks refer to the *informal communication system.* You may use that term if it makes you feel more comfortable, but it is still gossip in new wrappings and is still essential to understanding your organization. Gossip can be malicious, of course, and can be used for blackmail. But it can also be very helpful in understanding behavior to know that a colleague is going through marital stress, another has a child on drugs, one is trying to balance caring for a disabled parent, and still another handles an overloaded job and works against a dissertation deadline.

Getting Together to Get It Together

Everything said so far is summed up in the cardinal and triune rule of administration: communicate, communicate, communicate. There are thousands of ways to communicate, but I want to emphasize one that has been crucial to the functioning of my institution during my vice-presidential tenure: the weekly executive officers' meeting.

I have been fortunate in working with four presidents who saw the importance of meeting regularly to share troubles and triumphs, to quarrel in a civil way, and to make decisions. In nineteen years of sitting at the big table in the president's conference room, I have been stimulated, humbled, educated, praised, challenged, bored, and most certainly instructed. The important thing is that I have been informed and have had the opportunity to inform. The result of such interchange is that all the vice-presidents have been in a position at least to understand why a decision went a certain way, even if they did not necessarily agree. Another result has been that any of the vice-presidents could step into the job of any of the others and do it creditably from day one.

Note that the purpose of such meetings is not to take a vote, with the majority winning. To the contrary; as one president said, "The vote is ten ayes, one nay, and the nay has it." The purpose is to make consensual decisions, when possible, and to help the president make informed decisions, when necessary. I do not see how I could have done my job without this essential kind of communication. If you lack such an important opportunity, start campaigning for it now.

Epilogue

As you work with your president and your colleagues, as you teach and learn, as you follow and lead, and as you struggle with the myriad insoluble problems you face every day, just remember one important rule of life: no matter how bad your job is, someone else wants it.

References

Bennis, W. "The Dilemma at the Top: Followers Make Good Leaders." *New York Times,* Dec. 31, 1989, p. F-3.
Townsend, R. *Up the Organization.* New York: Knopf, 1970.

Ronald M. Brown is professor of higher educational administration at the University of Texas, Austin.

In this chapter, key faculty values, issues, and concerns are identified as they may affect the college or university political environment and, consequently, the work of the student affairs staff.

Key Academic Values and Issues

Paul A. Bloland

Student affairs administrators are always aware that they are playing on a larger field than that encompassed by their administrative portfolio. Certainly the teaching faculty looms large in that field, and it is a matter of no little concern to student affairs staff when it appears that faculty are at best seemingly uninterested in students and student life and at worst hostile to the extracurriculum and its protagonists. This all too pervasive indifference to values and programs that those in student affairs hold dear is not only often puzzling and frustrating but also contributes to a campus political climate that tends to undervalue student life and those who contribute to it. The concomitant attitudes may have a direct effect not only on the fiscal resources available to student affairs but also on the staff's ability to develop programs and policies affecting out-of-class student life or to enter into working relationships with faculty to enhance the educational environment of the institution. What is there about the faculty culture and value system that may, in part, explain these attitudes, and what can student affairs staff do to enlist faculty support and involvement in student life?

It is the purpose of this chapter to provide student affairs staff with a broadly framed picture of the world of the college and university faculty and the ways in which the pressures, concerns, and motivations inherent in that world may impinge on the mission of the student affairs division. Beginning with a brief discussion of institutional culture and the role of the faculty, this chapter will provide an overview of how faculty participation at the institutionwide, divisional, and departmental levels acts to influence the formal political process. The pressures implicit in the teaching, research, and service responsibilities of the faculty are identified, together with their influence on the nature and scope of faculty involvement in campus decision making and on faculty attitudes toward the student affairs function. A faculty view of student affairs is then presented, and a number of practical strategies for enlisting faculty support are identified.

University Culture and the Role of the Faculty

One cannot, of course, discuss the culture of higher education as if it were a single, monolithic entity. We have major research universities, community colleges, freestanding professional schools, denominational colleges, trade schools, and liberal arts colleges, to give but a glimpse of the often bewildering diversity that characterizes American postsecondary education today. However, most institutions are profoundly influenced by the ways in which they envision their missions. Does the college view itself primarily as a teaching institution, with its focus on the transmission of knowledge, or as a research institution devoted primarily to the generation of new knowledge? This is not to say, of course, that the teaching and research functions are not both embraced in varying degrees by many colleges and universities, but rather that they are all affected in some form or another by this bifurcation of role.

For example, the faculty role in the typical research university is quite different from that of faculty in teaching institutions. While both will be evaluated on their teaching performance, professors in the research university will also be subject to an ongoing evaluation by their peers, locally and nationally, of their research productivity. Although not by any means discouraged, research is not required by the teaching institution. As a result, faculty in these two different types of institutions will allocate their time differently between research and training.

Closely allied is the particular niche that the institution envisions itself as occupying or striving to fill. Is it international scholarly distinction? National prominence in professional education? An appeal to a particular religious denomination? A reputation for a strong liberal arts education? An opportunity for a low-cost and utilitarian urban education? An experimental approach to undergraduate education? The institution will tend to recruit and reward on the basis of a faculty member's contribution to that niche. The new faculty member quickly learns what will pay off in his or her college or university and begins to meet the unstated expectations of that environment.

Institutions of higher learning were first organized around teaching, and that function has remained at the heart of most institutional mission statements. The teaching/learning paradigm is the raison d'être of most higher education, and those who teach are implementing the central purpose of the college or university, carrying out the principal line function. It follows that most nonteaching roles are primarily supportive of the teaching function—that is, in administrative terminology, they are staff roles. Administrators may be essential, but they are not the reason why the college or university exists.

The Faculty in University Governance

Unlike the teaching faculty in elementary and secondary schools, who are often dominated by powerful administrators, university and college faculty have traditionally played a prominent role in decision making, particularly with respect to the academic program but certainly not limited to it. The faculty exercises its political muscle formally or bureaucratically, through an elaborate system of elected governing councils and appointed committees, or informally, through an even more complex if less charted system involving personal relationships, individual personality, political alliances, and acknowledged professional competence and prestige. The formal system of faculty governance may, in some institutions, have virtual veto power over administrative actions or appointments while in other colleges or universities it may function only as an ineffectual rubber stamp for administrative decisions. The vast majority of faculty senates and councils fall somewhere in between these two polarities, although, as Baldridge (1971) has pointed out, a mobilized faculty can, if necessary, exercise power by calling on the authority of professional knowledge or on such coercive tactics as strikes, class boycotts, or threats of bad publicity. Faculty participation in institutional governance typically takes place via several venues, ranging from the institutionwide level to the departmental level.

Institutionwide Governance

Most universities have a faculty governing group, usually called the faculty senate, with members elected by their colleagues to represent their interests with respect to the enactment of policies and programs that may affect them. The faculty senate will carry out its responsibilities through an executive committee, composed primarily of its officers, and through a committee system, with committees organized to address both senate housekeeping functions, such as an elections committee or a budget committee, and universitywide issues, such as faculty fringe benefits, approval of new courses and curricula, or faculty remuneration.

In the larger institutions, there will also be a university committee system with chairs and members appointed by the president and composed of faculty, staff, and student members. The administrative committees most often provide policy direction and consultation to administrative areas, such as student affairs, athletic affairs, or the university budget.

Both the faculty senate and the president's office may also appoint task- or crisis-oriented ad hoc committees or task forces to study and recommend an approach or resolution to a specific issue or problem not readily relegated to one of the standing committees. The ad hoc committee studies the problem, formulates a response for the approval of the appointing officer, and is then discharged once its job is completed.

In smaller colleges, there may be a representative body of faculty, administrators, and sometimes students that serves as an institutionwide policymaking and sounding board. Its function is still the same—to provide faculty and students with an opportunity for input into the institutional decision-making processes.

College Governance

In a university, each separate college or professional school may have its own elected representative body, known as a college or faculty council, whose functions are roughly the same as those of the institutionwide councils or senates. The college council serves as a policy board, advising the dean of the college on policy considerations and administrative issues, advancing faculty welfare, and operating through a committee system as well. Several of the standing committees of the college may be critical to the career of the individual faculty member, particularly those concerned with the salary merit system, promotion and tenure recommendations, or course and curriculum approval.

Departmental Governance

Partly administrative and partly policymaking, it is in the academic department that governance comes closest to affecting the day-to-day routine of individual faculty members, and it is with the department that faculty are most likely to identify themselves, not with the greater campus. The departmental chair may be elected by an advisory vote of the members of the department and confirmed or appointed directly by the dean. The departmental chair usually functions as the administrative head of the department and as a communications link between the departmental faculty and the administrators of the college, representing the concerns of the faculty to the dean, attending meetings with administrative officers and other chairs, and transmitting to faculty directives and issues raised by the dean.

The academic department has considerable autonomy within the college or professional school, often deciding what will be taught each term, when it will be taught and by whom, subject to the dictates of the college calendar and the general schedule-making rules and procedures. Faculty, participating together in department meetings or committees, may make decisions on such crucial issues and responsibilities as student admission standards, which students will be admitted and which rejected, which failing students should be dropped, what courses constitute a major or a minor, exceptions to departmental regulations, unusual expenditures in the budget, content of new courses, recommendations for prizes and awards, as well as financial aid and fellowships, to mention but a few of the myriad tasks that a department may assume.

The department is also the point at which faculty recruitment and recommendations for appointment, promotion, and tenure are first considered and initiated. Often operating through a search committee, departmental faculty conduct nationwide searches, sift through pools of candidates, and recommend to deans new candidates for appointment.

The next step for the department is to help the new faculty member (the new assistant professor in particular) survive for the first few years of appointment, while he or she and the department look each other over, to see if either is worth the investment of the up to six years it normally takes to achieve promotion to the next rank, associate professor, and the accompanying tenure.

Contrary to popular belief, the fledgling assistant professor is not necessarily given undesirable classes at undesirable times, overloaded with an excessive teaching load, or in other ways harassed by senior faculty. The new assistant professor, particularly in research institutions, represents not only a major recruiting investment but also the future hopes of the department for greater academic distinction, hopes that will not be realized if the neophyte is unable to be promoted or tenured. Consequently, the teaching load for new faculty in research universitites may be reduced for the first one or two years. They are discouraged from chairing doctoral committees and dissertations, dissuaded from getting involved in student activities and student life, and may be given such perquisites as research assistance and funds. Their time will be zealously protected by the department, to give them an opportunity to learn the ropes and get a research program under way. Senior faculty may conduct an annual review of the work of the assistant professors, to monitor their progress and give them advice and encouragement. With six years, at the most, to establish themselves before coming up for promotion, new assistant professors are under heavy pressure to succeed—success being defined in research institutions as concrete evidence (publication) that the initial promise is in the process of being fulfilled.

Many student affairs staff fail to understand why the award of tenure is so critical to the young faculty member. It is not just a matter of future job security—in academic circles, tenure means nothing less than career survival. Professors must either win tenure or leave their institutions. In short, they are essentially fired and must henceforth contend with explaining why they left their former colleges or universities without tenure. Rather than look for work in inferior institutions, they may leave academia altogether.

One would expect, given the extraordinary emphasis in the large research university on faculty research production, that every effort would be made to relieve the faculty member of extraneous duties or nonproductive routine. Such efforts are indeed made, by providing computer services, secretarial and clerical assistance, research help, sabbaticals, released time, and travel funds; but, all too often, these amenities are too limited and too spread out to be of real help. Two or three faculty members may share the services of one secretary. Research assistants are not provided except through personally negotiated research grants. Travel is restricted, and sabbaticals may be only a hope, but the faculty member is still expected to teach, provide service, and conduct research at a high level. Often faculty members must make up for institutional shortcomings by personal expenditures from their own salaries because, without the research record, there is little hope of advancement, annual salary increases, or peer recognition.

Given these imperatives, one can begin to understand that faculty may evaluate deans or departmental chairs on the extent to which they can provide resources and assistance that will facilitate faculty members' work while keeping bothersome routine and mundane tasks off their collective backs. Colleges and departments are always underfunded or believe they are underfunded, a restriction that attenuates the ability of the faculty to do their job, which, in turn, is vital to their own professional survival, if not to the institution.

The Faculty

Most student affairs staff have only a vague understanding of the work of the college or university professor. They are aware that it is difficult to find faculty members in their offices, that faculty may usually take a full day off each week, that they teach only a few hours each week, and that they never seem to find time for student activities. They are also aware that faculty may like them as people but may not hold their job functions or professional competence in very high esteem. What is there about the faculty role that may explain this profile?

One can begin by examining the reward structure, those activities that may result in a salary increase or a promotion, a powerful motivator. There are institutional imperatives that drive the reward structure. The teaching institution announces that it is concerned with the quality of the classroom and with the quality of the campus experience, but faculty may do scholarly work if they so choose. The research institution says that it is concerned equally with teaching, research, and service, although its reward structure clearly indicates that research is primary.

However, the typical faculty profile will call for equal doses of teaching and research and a lesser service requirement. The complete faculty member is the one who can do it all, who is able to perform at a high level in all three roles. Institutions will vary in the emphasis they place on each, but faculty quickly grasp the local norms of faculty productivity and evaluation.

Research

In the major, high-prestige universities, in those second-level institutions aspiring to their ranks, and in many other lesser institutions, faculty are expected to do research in their specialties and to publish it in the best journals in their fields. National visibility and reputation accrues to the faculty member, department, and institution through the recognition given the faculty member by publication in scholarly journals, books, and monographs. This external recognition supposedly draws able graduate students, research grants, and gift moneys and, in turn, provides the ruler by which the employing institution measures the faculty member's worth.

As Caplow and McGee (1958) have put it, the real strain for university professors lies in the fact that while they are hired and paid to teach, their worth to the institution is evaluated on how well they do what is essentially a voluntary part-time job that they have created for themselves—namely, research. This emphasis leads to faculty members' spending less and less time with students and colleagues in teaching and university service, and more and more time traveling off campus or in the laboratory or library. The ultimate prize is reached when the exceptional faculty member is allowed to drop all teaching and service responsibilities in order to devote that time to enhancing his or her research reputation.

As a result of these pressures, research faculty tend to be much more identified with the disciplines that are the source of their status than with the institutions that employ them. They become more mobile, ready and willing to leave for another college or university that makes them a better offer. Loyalty to the institution is not a strong point while service is equated with off-campus professional activities, and not with more parochial local needs and concerns.

While scholarly publication of research, theory, and ideas is the way in which faculty attempt to advance their professional reputations, it is not all that easy to get published. An article submitted to a peer-reviewed journal must be evaluated by a jury of experts on the topic under consideration and by the journal editor, who may reject it outright or return it with a request for revision, a process that may continue for months. If finally accepted, the article may undergo several more revisions before being published.

However, as faculty members view the scholarly expectations of their role, they see more than the timeworn "publish or perish" imperative; the phrase might as well read "publish *and* perish." Once published, an article or a book may be the subject of critical review and comment by fellow experts all over the country, and a reputation can be lost as well as won after publication. At the time a faculty member is evaluated by peers for promotion or tenure, the body of his or her published work is sent to some of the top figures in the discipline, who are asked to comment on the quality of the work and its contribution to the field. Sheer volume of production may be insufficient if the published work is judged to be superficial or insignificant. Poor reports from peer reviewers will not be helpful to the aspirant to tenure.

Even after tenure is secured, the pressure to publish, to achieve, is as relentless as ever for most. Not only does eventual promotion to full professor rest on the development of a national reputation through publication and professional activities, but the size of the annual merit increase is frequently contingent on continuing high production. Of course, their pride and sense of self-esteem will not permit most faculty to rest on their oars once tenured.

Given these concerns and incentives, is it any wonder that faculty must spend as much time as feasible in activities that build reputations? Anything else must be regarded as irrelevant or an imposition. One's valuable time is better spent on things that count.

Teaching

The teaching load will vary with the nature of the institution and the faculty member's other responsibilities, such as a special-projects assignment or election to a departmental chair, but may still range from one three-hour course per week to as much as fifteen hours of teaching each week. Faculty in research universities, particularly at the graduate level, tend to teach fewer hours per week than those in teaching institutions or those teaching undergraduate students. Each hour of classroom contact requires several hours of preparation time (yes, even experienced faculty must prepare for each class). Additional time is involved in supervising graduate students at the master's or doctoral levels, grading examinations and course papers, and keeping office hours, as well as in the personal and program advisement of students. All of these are generally considered to be teaching-related responsibilities. In addition, the recent literature that keeps flooding into the office must be reviewed for course or research relevance, and the total hours devoted to teaching may vary from twenty-five to forty hours per week.

Service

Service activities constitute a third area of faculty endeavor and, consequently, evaluation. While not considered as significant as research and teaching, service is nevertheless one of the major responsibilities of professors in both types of institutions, and faculty derive prestige and recognition from their participation. Working with student organizations is a recognized form of service, but, unfortunately, it does not carry the same potential for reward as involvement in a national professional organization or participation in campus or faculty governance or committee work.

Service responsibilities generally consist of active participation as an officer, committee member, chair, or journal editor in a professional association; institutional service in governance, ad hoc, and standing committees or election to the faculty senate at the universitywide or college level; and service in the department, departmental meetings, committees, interviewing of applicants, and the like. Some colleges and universities also look with favor on outside activities that represent the institution to the public, such as community activities, speaking engagements, and participation in local government. The amount of time devoted to service activities varies greatly, depending on the nature and extent of the faculty member's involvement. The president of a national professional association or scholarly society may devote so much time to the organization that he or she may be given released time (the course load may even be reduced by the dean because of the prestige accruing to the college). Another member of the department may simply participate in the routine departmental activities and duties expected of everyone. Faculty time devoted to service may range from five to twenty-five hours per week.

Faculty members may have to assign from thirty to sixty hours per week to teaching and service and still find additional time for research and scholarly activities. Because teaching and service responsibilities leave the faculty little flexibility (that is, classes meet at fixed times, office hours are kept at scheduled times, committees meet on a regular basis, and attendance at faculty meetings is expected), they must find time for such research activities as planning, grant writing, reviewing literature, conducting studies, analyzing data, and writing for publication, wherever and whenever they can. Because one can never do enough research or publishing, the work week of the faculty member can become staggering.

Related Issues

In spite of these demands, most faculty also have families and social lives, and may play golf or tennis on weekends for their mental and physical health which means that some compromises must be made, most often at the expense of research activities, because research and writing time is at the faculty person's discretion. However, this allocation of time may be costly because points scored in research count more than those accumulated in teaching and service. The conscientious faculty member finds himself or herself under constant pressure to achieve a great deal in a limited time and to produce work that must meet the qualitative standards of peers, locally and nationally.

As if meeting these taxing time constraints and peer standards were not enough, ethnic minority and women faculty members face additional expectations. For example, there still are not many minorities and women on faculties, particularly in research universities, and so, as exemplars and models of affirmative action, they may become more involved in campus activities and committee work than the typical faculty member. As Carpenter, Paterson, Kibler, and Paterson (1990, p. 209) have pointed out, minority faculty members are also in "incredibly high demand among minority students to serve as mentors, a function often underappreciated or totally unrecognized by the reward structure."

Although faculty are generally oriented toward their subject fields, having chosen teaching and research because of their deep interest in their disciplines, many also enjoy students and would become involved in student life if the personal cost were not too high. Unfortunately, it often is not feasible, particularly for young faculty members just launching their scholarly careers. Advising student organizations, student government, and student residences is not considered as meritorious as other types of service. To become involved with student affairs or student life is to make a considerable sacrifice, one that has little payoff in career advancement.

A Faculty View of Student Affairs

What are the sources of the typical faculty antipathy, if not hostility, toward student affairs? As described earlier, faculty simply do not have the time or energy to become involved in student life in any meaningful way, even if they should wish to participate. However, there are other factors that may contribute to student affairs' perceived lack of status in the eyes of the faculty.

Seen as an element of campus bureaucracy, student affairs shares with other administrative offices a low-key, passive resentment on the part of many faculty. For example, when the economic situation deteriorates, faculty tend to look outside their own departments to other departments that they perceive as commanding a disproportionate proportion of the budget, or to other schools and colleges—lacking in equivalent distinction, of course—that appear to get more funding than they deserve. The administrative offices commonly receive the most criticism, primarily for the perceived overstaffing, luxurious offices, and other unneeded amenities and privileges.

Under these conditions, student affairs becomes a primary target for several reasons: too much money goes to too many staff people who are not well trained, who are performing tasks not well understood by the faculty, or, if understood, are not seen as worth doing anyway. This view becomes exacerbated in times of financial exigency, and student affairs becomes very vulnerable to budget raids and cuts. Faculty can understand the need for the finance and accounting offices because that is where their checks come from. They can grasp the fund-raising function. That academic officers have a quasi-legitimate function goes without saying. But faculty ask, "Just what is it that these people in student affairs do that requires x percent of the annual budget?" Student affairs is seen as vulnerable competition for limited funds in times of budget cutbacks.

Historically, faculty have played an active role in both curricular and extracurricular education but, unfortunately, have since moved away from this broad definition of their educational responsibilities and no longer have much interest in it. Student affairs officers were appointed to fill the void left by faculty's lack of interest and have since functioned as partisans of the educational value of out-of-class life for students, described by the American Council on Education (1949) as a concern for the "whole student." As agents of what Brubacher and Rudy (1976) have termed "the reintegration of the curriculum and extracurriculum," student affairs professionals have developed a philosophy of higher education that emphasizes out-of-class learning as a significant element of the total higher education experience. Student affairs staff, being themselves products of the current system of higher education, fully recognize the primacy of cognitive learning in that system and want to be accepted as contributing members of it. But they offer as justification for membership in the academic community their interest and ability in noncognitive education, the affective domain, what Knapp (1962) has called "the character-developing function," a form of education that faculty neither understand nor respect.

As a result, the area of student affairs and its partisans, through much of the latter history of higher education, has been identified by the faculty as not particularly significant, as not counting for much in the scheme of things on campus. Fairly or not, to be involved with students and their somewhat juvenile activities is viewed by the academic professional as a lightweight occupation, of little consequence when compared to the laboratory and the world of ideas. Real learning occurs only in the classroom, and "other campus activities that divert students' time, energy, or attention away from their classwork are consequently viewed with suspicion" (Zeller, Hinni, and Eison, 1989, p. 52).

Student affairs officers have tended to be associated in the faculty mind with keeping order on campus and with an unfortunate preoccupation with the encouragement and supervision of such anti-intellectual activities as cheerleading or fraternities, activities that the faculty believes compete with the classroom for attention.

When faculty look at the academic credentials of student affairs staff, they see only the baccalaureate or master's degree, and that in professional education, rather than in an academic discipline to which they could more easily relate. Staff qualifications suffer in comparison to those of faculty, who have doctorates, do research, publish nationally, and perform the essential function of teaching. This perception places student affairs staff in a one-down position with respect to faculty from the start, and student affairs staff have some distance to travel if they are to improve their intellectual image with their faculty colleagues.

The academic functions, teaching and research, form the core of what the institution is all about. Everything else is regarded by the faculty as subordinate or extraneous to those functions, no matter how competently or professionally performed. As a result, as pointed out by Barr and Fried (1981, p. 88), faculty and student affairs administrators may "constitute two distinct subcultures on many campuses." An understanding of this reality is essential if student affairs staff are to deal realistically with its consequences.

Strategies for Working with Faculty

Although there are undeniable pressures on faculty, some of which may have a crucial impact on their careers, many faculty still want to be involved with student activities and student life, and many will make the necessary sacrifices because they believe that such involvement is an integral faculty responsibility, regardless of what the reward system maintains. They may share with student affairs staff a belief in the development of the whole student and believe that it is part of their responsibility as educators to lend their maturity and expertise to enhancing the quality of campus life or to creating a broadly defined cultural and intellectual environment in which student activities play a major role. These are the faculty who will be most interested in becoming involved.

Why involve faculty in student life and student affairs programs? As advisers to student organizations, they can provide a helpful liaison with the student affairs staff and, in many instances, provide a stabilizing and knowledgeable presence in student groups, a task that may otherwise have to be performed by an understaffed and overextended student affairs office. Faculty advisers are apt to be much more sensitive to the academic concomitants of student activities or institutional policies than student affairs people, unfortunately, and this perspective should be infused continually into all areas of student life. Student affairs divisions need friends and allies on campus to carry out their tasks. Working with faculty may greatly increase their understanding and appreciation of the student affairs function and at the same time reduce the traditional isolation and provincialism of student affairs people. Faculty are also in a position to advise student affairs staff on faculty and institutional issues that may affect student affairs.

There are some general concerns that should be kept in mind in working with faculty. The student affairs division needs to be seen as clearly involved in supporting the institutional mission and as sponsoring and encouraging programs of undeniable academic and intellectual worth. Staff should be wary of touting student development to faculty as the equivalent of intellectual development or as the sole justification for their programs because that tends to turn off faculty who are committed to other value systems. They should instead continually demonstrate how the student affairs division is essential to the mission of the college or university, not just by providing support services but also by developing mission-related programs and responsibilities, such as reducing student attrition, increasing ethnic and racial diversity on the campus, or changing the intellectual and cultural life of the campus. Staff members should employ the rhetoric of academe rather than the jargon of student affairs. By stressing the commonality of the interests student affairs staff have with faculty and implementing programs that reflect that commonality, the student affairs division can be viewed by faculty as a genuine partner in the academic enterprise.

Student Affairs Involvement with Faculty

It is important that student affairs staff relinquish their preoccupation with management and student activities and join with the faculty, so that they and their programs are visible partners in supporting academic and intellectual values and in implementing the academic mission. Staff should move into the faculty world through involvement in institutionwide committee participation, particularly on those committees that affect academic policy and programs, by becoming involved in research activities, perhaps as partners with faculty; by lunching often at the faculty club; by doing guest lecturing on campus, or by teaching or coteaching credit or noncredit courses; by earning the doctorate; by acquiring academic rank; and by participating in departmental meetings, seminars, guest lectures, and other faculty activities, as feasible and as they are welcome. Participation in faculty development programs may present yet another avenue for disseminating the student affairs message to faculty.

Involving Faculty in Student Affairs Programs

Student affairs staff, while recognizing the realities of the faculty career and its attendant time pressures, should not allow that recognition to deter them from encouraging the participation of individual faculty members in student life activities and organizations. Whether they will participate or not is their decision, but until faculty are approached, student affairs staff will never know of their interest.

There are a number of ways in which faculty can become involved in activities that complement the responsibilities of the student affairs division. Faculty may enjoy participation in student affairs advisory groups, such as the institution's policymaking committee on student affairs or student-faculty advisory committees to various service departments, such as student aid, admissions, athletic affairs, and residence halls. Many college teachers have become involved as resident faculty or mentors in residence halls. Faculty have traditionally served as advisers to campus organizations, usually without the mediation of the student affairs office. However, most faculty have little idea of what is entailed in advising a student organization, and so the advisory role can be made more effective by providing low-key training workshops and manuals. Faculty will not participate if the training is more trouble than it is worth. Programs should not be held on weekends; optional times and dates should be offered instead. Extensive publicity, follow-up, and personal contact should be provided, and the program should be substantive, not an oral reading of the standard procedures and policies.

Faculty should be involved in the planning stage of new programs and policy development. It is at this stage that their expertise and creativity may be most useful—few faculty want to be involved in the administration of an ongoing or standing program. A time-limited project or program may be ideal for faculty involvement with a goal and a foreseeable termination date, so that participation does not drag on and on.

Because faculty participation in student life is a form of voluntarism, with the commitment often serving as its own reward, it is important that student affairs staff take every opportunity to provide recognition to those faculty members who have set aside some of their time to serve students or assist the student affairs staff. Participation may do little to facilitate faculty promotion or award of tenure, but it is nevertheless a form of good campus citizenship. Letters of thanks should be written, with copies to the dean of the faculty member's school. Notable faculty contributions can be acknowledged via the campus newspaper and student award ceremonies. Invitations to special luncheons, receptions for visiting dignitaries, service on prestigious committees, seating in the president's box at football games, and off-campus retreats can make faculty engagement worthwhile.

Conclusion

The world of the collegiate Mr. Chips, if it ever existed, basically disappeared generations ago, about the time that American higher education began to reorganize along the lines of the German university model, roughly after the Civil War. The "character development" function was gradually dropped in favor of research and teaching and was picked up by administrative officers, the forerunners of today's student affairs staff, who believed that it was an important aspect of higher education. Today, character development has become student development, and it is the student affairs division that has taken on the student development role.

Nevertheless, there are many faculty who, in spite of the nature of the contemporary professoriate, understand the importance of defining education more broadly than simply as classroom-oriented learning. If approached by students or staff who possess an understanding of the nature of the faculty role and an appreciation of the pressures and rewards inherent in that role, many faculty will readily agree to become involved in student life. If such involvement is to continue, it must be professional, intellectually respectable, clearly defined, and duly appreciated. Student affairs staff will need to meet faculty more than halfway and maintain the lion's share of the initiative if the relationship is to succeed. However, if the partnership does succeed and faculty do become engaged in student life at a reasonable level, everyone wins—students, staff, and faculty—and a significant dimension is added to the quality of the campus experience of students.

References

American Council on Education. *The Student Personnel Point of View*. (Rev. ed.) Washington, D.C.: American Council on Education, 1949.

Baldridge, J. V. *Power and Conflict in the University*. New York: Wiley, 1971.

Barr, M., and Fried, J. "Facts, Feelings, and Academic Credit." In J. Fried (ed.), *Education for Student Development*. New Directions for Student Services, no. 15. San Francisco: Jossey-Bass, 1981.

Brubacher, J. S., and Rudy, W. *Higher Education in Transition*. (3rd ed.) New York: Harper & Row, 1976.

Caplow, T., and McGee, R. J. *The Academic Marketplace*. New York: Basic Books, 1958.

Carpenter, D. S., Paterson, B. G., Kibler, W. L., and Paterson, J. W. "What Price Faculty Involvement? The Case of the Research University." *NASPA Journal*, 1990, 27 (3), 206-212.

Knapp, R. "Changing Functions of the College Professor." In N. Sanford (ed.), *The American College*. New York: Wiley, 1962.

Zeller, W., Hinni, J., and Eison, J. "Creating Educational Partnerships Between Academic and Student Affairs." In D. C. Roberts (ed.), *Designing Campus Activities to Foster a Sense of Community*. New Directions for Student Services, no. 48. San Francisco: Jossey-Bass, 1989.

Paul A. Bloland is professor emeritus, former academic department chair, and former vice-president for student affairs at the University of Southern California.

Many program managers in student affairs bring methods and values from their graduate training and entry-level positions that do not adequately prepare them for the conflicting roles of middle management. Building alliances within a political perspective is an approach they can use to manage the dynamics of being caught in the middle and thereby more easily accomplish their goals.

The Middle Manager: Truly in the Middle

Herman Ellis, Jim Moon

This chapter is for both the chief student affairs officer and the program manager. It will assist chief student affairs officers to reacquaint themselves with the difficulties unique to the role of middle management, in order to assist their middle managers to become more effective. For the program manager, this chapter will address three types of role conflict experienced by middle managers—bureaucratic role ambiguity, professional role incongruence, and performance role discrepancy—and suggests strategies for improving effectiveness and peace of mind while working in the context of being in the middle. A discussion of the role of the middle manager is relevant to the issue of managing the politics of student affairs because program managers are in pivotal positions for ensuring that the visions, policies, and values of senior administrators are translated into effective services for students. Learning how the middle manager can understand and use a political perspective to manage his or her program will multiply the effectiveness of the chief student affairs officer and provide the middle manager with an opportunity to have more impact from a position within the organization that inherently does not have much autonomy.

Over the last thirty years, campus administrative positions have changed in response to the changes in higher education. Both the size of our campuses and the need to serve a more diverse and changing student population have increased. Therefore, the nature of services to meet the needs of students and larger campuses requires new methods of delivery, new organizational schemes, and expanded expertise. These changes have been the catalyst to evolve a new group of student affairs professionals—

NEW DIRECTIONS FOR STUDENT SERVICES, no. 55, Fall 1991 © Jossey-Bass Inc., Publishers   43 namely, the middle managers, who must have a repertoire of sophisticated administrative skills, as well as expertise in program areas.

The middle manager in student affairs will be defined as the person responsible for a program (such as placement, financial aid, and activities) or group of programs. The suggestions made in this chapter for ways of dealing with being in the middle are just as applicable to the front-line service provider as they are to the campus president, although the nuance and emphasis will differ. Each position has unique pressures coming from all sides, as well as equal claims on how tough it is to get the job done while being caught in the middle. The focus and context of this chapter, however, will be the program manager. This focus is warranted, because the middle management role is one for which most student affairs professionals are not well prepared, and, with increased knowledge, it is one area over which the middle manager can have considerable influence. Suggestions on how to obtain and use such influence will also be given.

The Role of the Middle Manager

There is general agreement that middle managers are people between the first level of supervisors and the top executives or vice-presidents. In a sense, they are the people in the middle between the front line and the executive decision makers. The term *middle management* refers to "group leaders responsible for carrying out and implementing top management decisions. They interpret policies and long-range goals and change them into instructions, then construct a framework that line supervisors can follow. There is responsibility for planning, organizing, budgeting, and authorizing the materials, equipment, personnel, and other facilities needed" (Place and Armstrong, 1975, p. 39).

In higher education, middle managers administer the operations of the institution. They make it go. As Couch (1979, p. 23) states, "the middle manager has to learn how to exercise influence and gain support, how to get a reasonable share of resources, and how to get cooperation from people even when there is nothing to give in return."

Forbes (1984) states that the middle management role suggests that middle managers have executive responsibility, are conduits for information flow, and have professional expertise. The middle managers are the anonymous leaders, the unheralded heroes who keep the institution functioning and determine institutional tone and style (Scott, 1978a).

These references by authors of organizational theory describe well the feeling of being caught in the middle experienced by program managers. The "caught in the middle" feeling faced by managers is illustrated nicely by commonly experienced situations. A housing director, trying to influence alcohol abuse in residence halls, is limited by university values of teaching responsibility, which includes giving students the opportunity to learn by making mistakes. The housing director must therefore balance the values of the institution with the practical knowledge of what happens when inexperienced young people first learn how much is enough by drinking too much. A career placement officer, trying to provide access for students to interview with recruiters of their choice, is confronted by other students who object to certain recruiters, such as the CIA. An alumni director is caught between an independent alumni association's effort to raise funds from alumni for a special project and the institution's preference to allow only the development officer to solicit funds for such projects. A student activities director is caught between teaching students the philosophy and practice of self-governance, on the one hand, and the campus administration's expectation that the director will influence and perhaps even control student government, on the other. These situations and many similar ones are commonly experienced by the program manager.

The difficulties that are part of being a middle manager have grown enormously since the student affairs profession expanded in the 1960s with the growth of higher education. Since the 1960s, moreover, the number and type of middle management positions have also increased, creating such management positions as director, associate director, associate dean, and coordinator. These positions are all middle management roles occupied by incumbents with little formal training in how to use the "middleness" of the role.

Middle managers have taken on even more responsibility as the task for implementing policies of the campus has fallen on their shoulders. For example, the current national discussion on the topic of returning American Indian remains and artifacts will result in institutional policies on individual campuses. How does the student activities director help the American Indian Club, a student organization, accept a policy that American Indian students feel does not go far enough in protecting the interests of the American Indian community? As institutions attempt to alter their enrollment patterns, how does the financial aid director help staff and students accept a policy that shifts the balance of the average financial aid package from grants to loans, so that another portion of the student body receives aid packages with more grants than loans? The dilemmas posed by these questions are typical of the fallout created by institutional policies and test the timbre of middle managers who have responsibility to make things work.

Being caught in the middle distresses some middle managers, while others thrive on the constantly changing variety of challenges that the role presents. The remainder of this chapter provides middle managers on both ends of this spectrum with ideas for how to do their jobs better.

Role Development: A Challenge for Middle Management

Social scientists describe two kinds of roles: ascribed and achieved (Kraus, 1983). We have no control over ascribed roles, such as age, sex, and ethnicity. They are assigned without reference to individual differences, interests, and talents. Achieved roles, by contrast, are those positions filled through individual effort and, in theory, are chosen and personally controlled. Even though the role of the middle manager is an achieved one, it primarily responds to the needs of staff or to the policy and direction of senior administrators. Therefore, paradoxically, it is not primarily personally controlled.

The actual role of the middle manager is not clear, even though it regularly conforms to organizational circumstances. Role messages sent to midlevel managers, in both direct and indirect ways, create a role set. The perceptions of the role messages received may differ significantly from those sent, which may result in conflict. Role development in such instances is hampered by mixed messages. These mixed messages may result in ambiguity. Since most people find ambiguity stressful, the first problem for the middle manager to address is role clarification, by analyzing role ambiguities. Three types of role conflict experienced by the middle manager are bureaucratic ambiguity, professional incongruence, and performance discrepancy (Corwin, 1960).

Bureaucratic Ambiguity. This role conflict is inherent in the position itself and its place in the organizational hierarchy. An example of role ambiguity may be when a director of one unit reports through a director of another, unrelated unit. To identify the degree of bureaucratic ambiguity is to ask whether the organizational structure facilitates or impedes performance. Does the organizational structure facilitate collegial performance, attitudes, and collaborative practice? Is the university's environment cooperative, fair, caring, and characterized by the involvement of professional staff in decision making (Austin, 1985)? To the extent that these questions are answered in the affirmative, role ambiguity from the bureaucracy will be minimized.

Bureaucratic role ambiguity can only be eased, not eliminated. If the organization is dysfunctional, the central administration must address this issue. Multilevel discussion and input are very important, but the responsibility for addressing the problems caused by bureaucratic role ambiguity must be initiated at the top of the organization. If the middle manager finds bureaucratic role ambiguity pervasive, and the central administration is not addressing such problems as sphere of authority, accountability, cooperation, and competition, then a request for review, clarification, and restructuring may be desirable. At the same time, it is appropriate to identify and suggest ways to correct structural inconsistencies that are barriers to role clarification. These actions can reduce the stress and conflict caused by bureaucratic role ambiguity. If nothing else, it will bring to light the need for change within the organizational structure.

Professional Incongruence. This conflict is essentially internally driven and derives from self-perception based on one's values. Moving into a middle management position with broad responsibilities means shifting from a specialist to a managerial role. While most individuals have achieved expertise within a professional area, the middle manager may find himself or herself working in areas where others have the professional expertise. Thus the practitioner within one's unit may challenge, overtly or covertly, the manager's understanding of the real day-to-day problems in the delivery of services. Managers may feel vulnerable to such challenges. Further, the middle manager typically has less direct student contact than others within the unit, with the result that immediate feedback to the manager from direct student exchange is dramatically reduced. The lack of direct feedback may cause some discomfort within the middle manager.

Professional role incongruence is also felt by middle managers as they act as staff to senior administrators, who are likely to demand social distance and respect for their authority while providing only minimum recognition. At the same time, managers act as team leaders for their staffs. Therefore, management styles of middle managers must be adaptable to the needs of persons to whom they report and to those of the staff who report to them. The incongruities of behavioral expectations are apparent and potentially place a large strain on the middle manager.

One way professional role incongruence is dealt with is to accept that what management is trying to do is not in conflict with what front-line service providers are trying to do. Another way is to establish new links and networking with those in similar roles. Resolution of professional role incongruence is a continuous process. As such, the initial step toward resolution requires managers to resist suppressing their own professional values and image conflicts and to discuss them with colleagues and mentors, to develop a balance. By accepting the role of the middle manager and valuing and managing it, the middle manager's supervisors and those supervised will respect the middle manager's ability to work in the middle.

Performance Discrepancy. Performance role discrepancy and ambiguity for middle managers are the areas of confusion most indicative of unused or misused human relations skills. Due to inexperience or lack of sufficient knowledge and preparation, performance ambiguity is essentially functional by nature. If managers do not have the tools, techniques, and skills to handle the responsibilities, tasks may not get done effectively or efficiently. Mastering management techniques and skills can ease performance role discrepancy if middle managers use those skills most appropriate to the situation. The skills and techniques of management can be taught, but only in principle. They must be learned but can be learned only through guided practice, trial and error, modification and adaptation, and integration of the concepts of management, in the broadest sense of the word. In the actual performance of the middle manager, interpersonal skills are most crucial for easing performance role discrepancy.

These three types of role conflict can be a source of great discomfort and stress for the middle manager. A description of them has been included to give program managers some theoretical basis for understanding the dynamics that may hinder them as they work to attain their goals.

Lack of Autonomy and Validation for the Middle Manager's Role

Autonomy is defined by Hackman and Oldham (1980, p. 80) as "the degree to which the job provides substantial freedom, independence, and discretion to the individual scheduling the work and in determining the procedures to be used in carrying it out." Scott (1978a, p. 26) found "opportunities to act independently" an area of high satisfaction among the administrators he studied. Kohn (1976) has emphasized that control over one's work is a critical variable for employees in many workplaces. Similarly, Super and Hall (1978) postulate that career satisfaction is influenced positively by autonomy in conducting one's responsibilities, a sense of challenge in the work, and appropriate and sufficient rewards.

Since middle managers make decisions on the basis of the guidelines of senior administrators and the policies of institutions, they are perceived as having little autonomy over the institutional environment. The literature on middle managers includes references to the stepsister status (Thomas, 1978) accorded them by senior administrators and faculty. While being considered experts off campus, middle managers are often ignored on campus. They bear specialized expertise and information that may be ignored by policymakers (Scott, 1977, 1978a, 1978b). They express pride in their institutions but do not feel appreciated by them (Thomas, 1978). A feeling of powerlessness tends to encourage middle managers to become rules-minded and defensive about their domain. However, as a coping mechanism, it appears that middle managers receive satisfaction from autonomy within their own areas of responsibility, rather than expecting a strong role in the decision-making process at the senior level. Seeking autonomy can, however, contribute to territoriality, which can be troublesome for the chief student affairs officer.

It should be noted that senior administrators are extremely dependent on middle managers for getting the job done and serving as communications links with the program staff. As a result, program managers can be either assets or liabilities to their vice-presidents, depending on what the managers choose to focus on and how they screen information. Therefore, while middle managers may not feel much autonomy, they are in an important position to influence what gets accomplished.

One of the most significant acts of a chief student affairs officer in the supervision of middle managers is to provide recognition for growth and accomplishment. The literature indicates that recognition for what one does is frequently cited as being critical to job satisfaction. Chief student affairs officers should remember the importance of coaching and encouraging high staff performance. The impact of a personal note or telephone call of appreciation is very powerful. Encouragement can reaffirm what is important, provide motivation for continued achievement, and give some feeling of autonomy to the individual. The use of personal recognition is a key to success for both the senior administrator and the program manager.

Building Alliances: The Next Step

In addition to providing recognition and encouragement, vice-presidents can help their program managers by introducing them to the value of building alliances. As noted earlier, the role of middle managers is only partially self-controlled as they react to the needs of senior administrators and the staff who report to them. It is important to minimize this lack of control because managers have responsibility for implementing policy and need as much autonomy as possible to do so. One use of this autonomy, and a way to offset some of the lack of control experienced by them, is to acquire expertise in the art of building alliances. To do so means making contacts, linking people with ideas, getting and giving information, and giving support to the projects of others.

In the last several years, this process has been referred to as *networking*. However, for program directors, there is the need to go beyond networking if they are to survive and succeed in the active and fast-paced environment of higher education administration, where competing priorities seek limited institutional resources and valuing. Thus, the logical next step after networking is alliance building.

It is traditional for the helping professional to maintain distance from political processes and activities on campus. Being political may feel unethical and contradictory because it is often seen as manipulative. Program directors and chief student affairs officers have been nurtured and rewarded for educating students and providing competent services. They have not been encouraged or rewarded for being political. The apolitical perspective may still serve first- and second-line direct service providers well. However, when one becomes a middle manager, additional perspectives and skills must be used to successfully function as a member of the administrative team responsible for institutional management. The diverse and intense needs of student bodies, the complex legal environment of colleges and universities, and the high expectations held by students, faculty, parents, governing boards, alumni, and the public at large require a sophisticated understanding of how such interests and expectations interact and how one can respond in turn to affect those interests and expectations in a timely and productive fashion. One resource that the middle manager can employ is the political perspective. An important methodology that comes from this perspective is alliance building.

In building alliances, middle managers structure around themselves the kinds of people and personal allegiances necessary to achieve the goals they have set. It is critical to remember that these alliances are made up of relationships with people; therefore, alliance building must be based on reciprocal trust and respect. Middle managers must recognize their own abilities and determine how they can contribute to others. They must give their talents and resources to others in exchange for support.

Once a middle manager has an effective working knowledge of how to use an alliance system, it will develop into a solid foundation from which the middle manager can move toward more personal control, thereby maximizing the use of his or her own skills and talents toward accomplishing the goals that define success. One of the payoffs of using an effective system of alliances is the ability to consciously and intentionally share, both with the senior administration and one's staff, one's vision for the institution and the program. A support network can provide the manager with information, emotional support, contacts, role models, and the confidence he or she needs. Building alliances will help the middle manager implement a plan of action.

How to Build Alliances. The first and most important alliance-building strategy is developing mentor relationships with a few trusted and respected persons. One's primary mentor will likely be the traditional, experienced, and wise professional. This relationship will provide insight into the organizational, political, and historical dynamics of the institution and should provide information on which hoops to jump through and which to simply walk around. The primary mentor should be someone who has stronger credibility within the institution and someone who is willing to give guidance, especially in the case of a new professional or one who is new at the institution.

Perhaps as important as having a primary mentor is developing a collaborative relationship with colleagues in student affairs. One of these should be with a peer, such as a fellow program manager, and one with a front-line service provider. The first of these can provide insight into the dynamics of the institution from a perspective within the organizational structure and from a position similar to that of the program manager. This perspective is needed during times of high intensity caused by work overload, program traumas, or personal crises, which can easily affect one's ability to think clearly. The collaborative relationship with a front-line service provider is important in staying current on the emerging needs and values of the various subgroups within the student body. In addition, it is essential for the program manager to constantly remember what it is like to work directly with students. As the need exists, and depending on one's ability to manage more collaborative relationships, it is worthwhile to consider additional collaborative relationships with those who have expertise, skills, or values very different from one's own.

The purpose of developing such relationships is to provide the program manager with as comprehensive a view as possible, not only of the institution within which he or she works but also of the world and student affairs services, as seen by the student body, faculty, and staff. It is easy to allow preferred methods of approaching tasks to seductively reinforce one's belief that these approaches are the best ways of doing things. Actively consulting with others who have different viewpoints also helps to counteract the insulation that can easily occur without such exchanges. Middle managers must hone their observational skills as a way to gain information about how things work and to hear what students are telling the institution about their needs.

Understanding and learning how to use the politics of the campus can assist in better management of one's own programs. As noted earlier, being political or viewing the institution from a political perspective, has generally been anathema within the helping climate of the student affairs profession. Historically, being political has been the responsibility of the senior campus administrators. However, not to include the political perspective in one's repertoire of analytical skills and operating strategies is to operate without the full range of tools available.

Since the use of political views and strategies has generally been distasteful to the student affairs professional, it may be useful to redefine the term *politics* by describing it as how individuals behave toward one another in their efforts to accomplish both common and divergent goals. As a result of the redefinition, it can be noted that student affairs personnel are currently and actively involved in politics on campus. For example, helping a student develop strategies for working through a roommate conflict, preparing for job interviews, acquiring financial resources needed to obtain an education, working through a conflict with a colleague, preparing a professional development plan, and developing strategies for securing resources to enhance program goals are ways student affairs personnel are involved in the political process. Therefore, since the program manager does and can use political perspectives and methods, it is important to recognize, articulate, and use them more intentionally to achieve program success.

Alliance-Building Characteristics. The following contribute to successful alliance building by middle managers. The first one is the most important, the skill on which all other alliance-building strategies are based.

Interpersonal Skills. These are the ability to develop rapport, listen well, develop trust and mutual respect, read between the lines and be an effective negotiator and problem solver. Interpersonal skills are most productive when used with other skills, such as keeping perspective, treating others as you would like to be treated, having patience, being flexible, and maintaining a sense of humor.

Competence in Primary Program Area. While employing the strategies suggested in this volume will enhance the perception of an administrator's competence, the middle manager must have a track record of successfully managing and directing the program for which he or she is responsible. This includes demonstrated professional expertise in the program area, as well as success in the achievement of specific program goals. The credibility one gains from performance is a prerequisite for building alliances. Success with alliance building can also enhance the middle manager's ability to successfully manage his or her program during times of broad changes in the institution, political crossfire, and program threats caused by budget cutbacks. Established alliances will minimize the impact to one's program during difficult times.

Professional Reputation. By demonstrating strong interpersonal skills and competence in a program speciality, one is able to create and maintain a strong, positive, professional reputation and will give others confidence in the middle manager's abilities, judgment, and commitments. Since a positive reputation is also a requirement for significant career advancement, one must develop a sound reputation and credibility early in one's career and systematically maintain them.

Big-Picture Perspective. It is crucial to have a big-picture perspective. Most middle managers must move back and forth between functions that require narrowly prescribed skills, on the one hand, and that demand attention to broader divisional or institutional concerns, on the other. One important test for the middle manager is to be consistent yet flexible enough in style to adapt to the changing needs of the individual department and the institution in general. Middle managers must be able to see beyond their units and help provide leadership and support for the goals of the division or institution. The middle manager must have the ability to shift mental and emotional gears quickly, from meeting the needs of individual units to those of the larger arena of institutional management and back again.

Self-Assurance. In the role of staff to senior administrators, middle managers must be willing to accept the notion that ideas generated by them may be credited to senior administrators. Middle managers must not take rejection of or disagreement with their ideas or proposals personally and must be able to have their work rejected, modified, or claimed by someone else. They must be able to cope with being only a piece of the problem-solving effort for which the institution holds them accountable. In general, one cannot depend on getting recognition from the bureaucracy, and so being able to separate professional identity from personal identity is critical.

Professionalism. Ethics, integrity, good work, and a deep regard for students are the keystones here.

Care and Limitations. Managers who are most successful have such deep regard for students that even when resources are limited they still find a way to provide good services.

The Golden Rule. Successful managers treat others as they themselves would like to be treated. Most hold this attitude for those they supervise but at times forget that the principle is also applicable to the chief student affairs officer. Middle managers must support their bosses in public, keep them informed to avoid unnecessary surprises, be aware of competing demands and priorities for their time and resources, have an appreciation for their breadth of responsibility, and be cognizant of the forces with which chief student affairs officers must contend.

Additional Important Characteristics. Have a sense of humor—it is stress-relieving and essential for living with the many contradictory expectations and competing priorities of your work. Be patient—our institutions and world are now so complex, it simply takes longer to accomplish goals. On the interpersonal level, the admonition of not judging another until you have walked a mile in his or her shoes is a good reminder. Be smart—it is helpful to have a sixth sense to help read between the lines and stay focused on important issues. One needs to choose battles carefully. Very few battles in one's career are worth loss of employment. The real test of one's ability is to pick battles where a win will enhance both the program and one's reputation. Be flexible—including the capacity to choose wisely between meeting the needs of the program and meeting those of the institution, to know how and when to place more emphasis on one's own unit, the division, or the campus, and to maintain a dual unit/institution perspective. Relieve stress (short and long term)—the need to manage stress is self-evident but rarely met. Strategies for stress relief within the workday as well as the annual vacation are essential to being productive professionally.

Conclusion

The middle manager in student affairs typically experiences three types of role conflicts. These managers have often been limited by training and the values of the profession to focus on the delivery of services and development of students. In recent years, networking has been articulated within the profession as a strategy to pursue program goals more effectively, assist with institutional complexities, and provide personal support to enhance personal performance.

The student affairs program director in the role of a middle manager needs to do more than networking in order to be successful in contemporary higher education. Building alliances within a political perspective is one of the methods available to program directors. Such a perspective has frequently been anathema to many student affairs professionals. However, in order to work successfully in today's sophisticated administrative environment, the political perspective and the use of alliances are critical to quality performance and advancement.

References

Austin, A. E. "Factors Contributing to Job Satisfaction of University Midlevel Administrators." Paper presented at the annual meeting of the Association for the Study of Higher Education, Chicago, Illinois, March 1985.

Corwin, R. G. "Role Conception and Mobility Aspirations: A Study in the Formation and Transformation of Nursing Identities." Unpublished doctoral dissertation, University of Minnesota, 1960.

Couch, P. "Learning to Be a Middle Manager." *Business Horizons,* 1979, *22,* 33–41.

Forbes, O. Z. "The Middle Management Professional." *Career Perspectives in Student Affairs,* 1984, *1,* 39–46.

Hackman, J. R., and Oldham, G. R. *Work Redesign.* Reading, Mass.: Addison-Wesley, 1980.

Kohn, M. L. "Occupational Structure and Alienation." *American Journal of Sociology,* 1976, *82,* 111–130.

Kraus, J. D., Jr. "Middle Management in Higher Education: A Dog's Life?" *Journal of the College and University Personnel Association,* 1983, *34* (4), 29–35.

Place, I., and Armstrong, A. *Management Careers for Women.* Louisville, Ky.: VGM Career Series, 1975.

Scott, R. A. "Misdirected Missionaries: Personnel Officers in Academe." Speech presented at the annual meeting of the College and University Personnel Association, Cincinnati, Ohio, October 1977.

Scott, R. A. *Squires and Yeomen: Collegiate Middle Managers and Their Organizations.* ERIC/Higher Education Research Report no. 7. Washington, D.C.: American Association of Higher Education, 1978a.

Scott, R. A. "Yeast for the Yeomen, Sauce for the Squires: Incentives for Improving Administrative Competence and Performance." Paper presented to the National Assembly of the American Association of University Administrators, Chicago, 1978b.

Super, D. C., and Hall, D. T. "Career Development: Exploration and Planning." *Annual Review of Psychology,* 1978, *29,* 333–372.

Thomas, G. S. "Organizational Commitment: Sources and Implications for the Development of Middle Managers." Unpublished doctoral dissertation, Cornell University, 1978.

Herman Ellis is assistant vice-president for student life at California State University, Chico.

Jim Moon is associate vice-president for student affairs at California State University, Chico.

While the political activities of the small college and religious institution occur in a unique cultural context, they cannot be avoided. Politics and power can best be understood in ways that contribute to, rather than detract from, the work of those in student affairs in these kinds of institutions.

Small Colleges and Religious Institutions: Special Issues

Daryl G. Smith

Many student affairs professionals, particularly those in small colleges and in religious institutions, often find themselves loath to acknowledge the political dimensions of their organizations. This reluctance to deal with issues of politics and power is common in many other organizations but is exacerbated in these institutions, in part because of perceptions of fundamental tension between conventional conceptions of politics and power and the unique nature of the institutions. The chapter will begin with a discussion of politics and power, followed by a description of some of those distinctive characteristics of small colleges and religious institutions that are particularly relevant to political issues on campus. This chapter will suggest that political activity of some kind will certainly play a role in the life of an involved student affairs administrator and that conceptions of politics and power can best be understood in ways that contribute to, rather than detract from, the work of those in student affairs in small colleges and religious institutions.

Politics and Power

If political behaviors are defined as those designed to influence or determine institutional policy and direction, as suggested in Chapter One, then most of our activities could be defined as political. Why, then, is there a problem when we begin to discuss the politics of organizations? In contrast to other ways of looking at organizations, the political model suggests a number of characteristics that highlight conflict and competition for resources. Viewing organizations through this lens suggests that there are a variety of groups and subgroups within the college or university, each with its own goals for itself and the organization and each attempting to make its own views and needs heard. Like many political assemblies, decision-making bodies typically include representatives of relevant groups, and the process may well focus on the resolution of competing perspectives through voting or through compromise. Political models of organizations acknowledge, therefore, that decision making is often the result of competing pressures of various interest groups for the allocation of resources. Conflict may result from differences in goals and priorities about important issues.

The literature now emerging on the politics of organizations suggests four conditions that are likely to facilitate the presence of political activities and introduce power as a central consideration: interdependence of authority, important issues, scarcity of resources, and decentralization of decision making (Baldridge, 1971; Pfeffer, 1981). Interdependence is the degree to which the desired change rests on the cooperation of others. Student affairs professionals desiring, for example, to improve the campus climate, or advising, or orientation invariably find themselves in situations that require the cooperation of others. Authority for change does not usually rest with one person or one office. The second condition requires that the issues be seen as important. Space, money, new programs, and specific policies will take on political significance when they are perceived to be important. If no one cares, then one can do almost anything. The issue of perceived importance is critical. What to one person may be a relatively simple decision and therefore may require little consultation may in fact be seen as a major decision leading to significant campus conflict. Knowing where the land mines are is one of the best rationales for being involved with a wide variety of constituencies on campus. Scarcity of resources is the third condition. Very simply, if there are enough resources (space, money, positions, and so on) there will be less political juggling for those resources. The last condition involves some decentralization of decision making. On most campuses, there are layers and layers of decision points, which create many opportunities to attempt to influence decisions and many opportunities for differences of opinion to emerge. Since these four conditions are met in most if not all our institutions, some aspects of the political model will occur on the campus.

At worst, these variables can be the elements of conflict. Even in small colleges and religious institutions, where there is potential for greater agreement about overarching mission and goals, there are often major disagreements about the means to those goals, competing perceptions about priorities, and conflicts concerning the allocation of resources.

Inevitably, then, discussions about the politics of a campus are directed to questions about power. Indeed, power, as defined by Appleton in Chapter One, is an essential ingredient of the political process. Yet understanding of the concept of power presents fundamental problems for many persons and institutions. In much of the traditional literature, power has been defined as "the ability of A to get B to do something that B *would not otherwise have done*" (Dahl, 1957, pp. 202–203; emphasis added). This particular understanding of power and the politics of power is really a view of coercive power. To the degree that we assume this kind of power in our discussions about decision making, it is no wonder that many in student affairs and other, more humanistically oriented, fields shy away from the fray. Clearly, coercive power is only one of several forms of power and by no means the most common. A more realistic notion of power is power as the ability to manage resources to create change. Having power, then, is having the ability to influence change. The source of power, in this sense, may come from one's position, access to positions of power, or budget control—opportunities that are limited to a select few. More often than not, it comes from other resources, such as information, expertise, having a constituency, being part of a coalition, having credibility, having a history with the institution, or having time to put into a project. In thinking about power in this way, an effective administrator is more likely to have more power than is often used. Power is not a limited quantity and can be expanded by sharing. The term *empowerment* is more common now in the management literature (Block, 1987).

Issues of politics and power can be construed in one way, as some kind of negative but inevitable part of functioning in an organization: combative, manipulative, destructive, and coercive. Alternatively, they can be viewed, from a human relations perspective, as the bringing together of diverse points of view to come to decisions. Student affairs professionals are traditionally process-oriented, trained to develop equitable and sensitive processes for the resolution of conflict and for decision making. Each issue on our campus—if it is significantly important, if we cannot resolve it ourselves, and if we have limited resources—requires our being able to see the variety of perspectives involved and developing processes by which solutions are reached. Whether we do this in the context of disagreement among student groups, roommates, or staff colleagues, we are engaged in a political process. When the issues are seen in this way, the student affairs professional has a great deal to contribute to the political dimension of our institutions. This can be a great source of power in these unique kinds of institutions, where resolution of conflict without destructive consequences is a value and where the ethos is tension with a political process.

The Distinctive Character of Small Colleges and Religious Institutions

Within the category of small colleges and religious institutions, there is an enormous variety that makes generalizations somewhat risky. Included would be small private institutions of two hundred students, as well as large Catholic institutions of many thousands. Even within small institutions, the varieties of philosophy, culture, and purpose can be great. Yet the vast majority of these institutions are small and are likely to have characteristics related both to size and to mission (Astin and Lee, 1972; Pace, 1974; Clark, 1972).

Independence. One virtually uniform characteristic of these institutions is that they are independent, as opposed to publicly supported. As a result, decision making is most often contained within groups and individuals more directly associated with the campus and, indeed, often on or near campus. Religious institutions that are accountable to church organizations may encounter some loss of control over aspects of decision making similar to that experienced by public institutions, but often there may be more shared purpose than might be typically true of a state university accountable to a legislative body. While being an independent institution may limit the number of groups competing for resources and attention, it by no means eliminates the political elements of decision making; the four conditions for the presence of political issues are present on virtually all campuses. On some campuses, decision making may be more hierarchical and less decentralized, but on most the nature of the academic enterprise, tenure, and faculty roles in governance means that decision making is shared across many groups.

Size. Many of these institutions are small, and size has a significant impact on the nature of decision making at all levels (Blau, 1970; Katz and Kahn, 1978). As organizations grow, there is less direct access to decision making and decision makers. On small campuses, there is often more opportunity for direct access to members of the board of trustees and even donors, not only for senior administrators but for staff members, faculty, and students as well. Not surprisingly, this contact is more often likely to be social on a smaller campus than would be true on a larger campus.

Accuracy of communications is likely to increase as size decreases. On smaller campuses, the opportunities for face-to-face communication among a wide variety of constituencies is much greater and more encouraged than on larger campuses, where contact is more often managed and decided by status or role.

It is much more difficult on large campuses to integrate and make full use of the skills of staff, faculty, and students. Indeed, on smaller campuses, a condition of understaffing often exists, in which there are too few people for the jobs to be done. The result is the necessity of greater participation by more members of the community, development of new skills, close cooperation, and more direct exposure to a variety of experiences. There are many more opportunities on smaller campuses to be a generalist, to move among roles, and to take on several roles at once (Barker and Gump, 1964).

Smaller campuses may have less variety of offerings and opportunities for staff, students, and faculty. The research by Barker and Gump (1964) has indicated, however, that on such campuses people tend to take more advantage of the opportunities present. In larger institutions, people tend to specialize more in selecting the people and activities with which they associate. That is more difficult to do on a smaller campus.

Increasing size can lead to the use of more rules and procedures, less face-to-face interaction, and fewer shared values. Smaller institutions tend to be less differentiated and more holistic, somewhat lessening the numbers of groups fighting for representation and reducing the kinds of fundamental differences that can make compromise or resolution of conflict difficult.

Mission. Small colleges and religious institutions tend to have missions that are more likely to bring diverse constituencies into agreement, out of concern for overarching goals. Moreover, these goals are much more likely to be highly compatible with and supportive of the concerns of student affairs. The denominational college is apt to strongly articulate concerns for the whole student, student character, and values. Many small colleges are relatively clear about their focus on teaching and learning and about the importance of student life. These campuses are often heavily residential and value and expect faculty participation in the lives and activities of students. Recent studies of faculty attitudes and values, for example, support the notion that in denominational and liberal arts colleges, faculty are more likely to be willing to take an active role on campus, to value teaching, to be more involved with students, and to experience a stronger sense of community (Boyer, 1989). While this perspective suggests that there is more of a focused mission, it is important not to oversimplify the complexity of agreeing on goals and purposes, even on these campuses. Even when global language can be readily accommodated, specific operational language may immediately produce differences of opinion. From a political perspective, there is more opportunity to approach the topic of shared values and mission at these institutions than at almost any other kind. Nevertheless, political issues do arise that are unique to these institutions and therefore present more of a challenge.

Challenges

The organizational culture and mythology of these institutions may place such a strong value on language concerning community, shared values, and even consensus that it may be more difficult to approach conflicts and disagreements. As a result, even as one pays attention to political issues it may be detrimental to be perceived as political.

There is also a challenge in being understaffed and, often, "underresourced." Every small institution is performing many of the same functions as larger campuses, but with much more limited resources. The director of student activities may also be the housing director. On some very small campuses, the dean of students, the registrar, and the financial aid director are the same person.

There are numerous other opportunities to be overloaded in these kinds of institutions. There are often many demands to participate in a much wider range of activities, both formal and social, inside and outside the student affairs area. Institutions in small towns often demand more community participation as well. Moreover, some denominational colleges expect extensive participation in religious and social activities on the part of staff and faculty and their families.

There is an absolute necessity on these campuses that student affairs professionals connect to the academic or church values of the institution. That does not mean that a person must be of the same faith or background, however. On a small campus, where one is more apt to be more visible and known, one cannot afford to be seen as having a philosophy totally unconnected to the prevailing culture and values of the institution.

In many small and, particularly, denominational institutions, one may have to recognize that some individuals or groups are more centrally involved with certain kinds of decisions. Not to have influence with such persons or groups would severely limit one's access to decision making. Being on the margins may be very problematic in such places, regardless of the reason for one's marginal position.

In such institutions, there is a great deal of informal interaction and informal decision making. While it is not often easy to articulate a clear decision-making process on many campuses, it can be particularly difficult on small campuses, where there may be a significant disjuncture between the formal and the informal (and sometimes real) decision procedures. Informality and lack of clarity require that administrators know what is going on in the entire institution.

Another challenge for student affairs in small colleges and religious institutions is that the student affairs area is often the object of a great deal of scrutiny. Faculty, other administrative officers, parents, and board members are often very involved in campus life and are likely to have opinions on the way things should be done. The result is even less control over decisions than might be the case on larger campuses.

There is a great risk in assuming that because an institution is small or shares certain values, it is simpler to lead or manage. In these institutions, the level of complexity is increased not because of size but because many more individuals and groups perceive that they should be involved, because there is more personal investment in decisions, because the absence of flexibility in allocating resources places great strain on budget matters, and because the institution struggles to participate in the increasing sophistication of higher education, with proportionately fewer resources to accomplish similar goals.

Because the campus culture may be more focused and intense, one of the elements of success in being able to participate effectively in campus decision making may be the degree to which one is perceived to fit the culture of the campus. Without that, efforts to make improvements or changes may be perceived as unsuitable for the institution. This can be a great challenge on campuses where effectiveness may be measured not by commitment of time and effort or by effectiveness but by loyalty.

Opportunities to Effect Change

In smaller colleges and religious institutions where teaching, learning, and all of student life are central elements of the institutional mission, people and connections to people form the basis of power. Student affairs personnel on such campuses have the potential to be central to the political process, rather than marginal to it. The challenge is to know how, where, and when to garner resources to use that position for the good of the institution, its educational mission, and for students themselves.

Understanding the Culture of the Institution. The culture of an organization influences the decision-making process. Student affairs professionals must be very sensitive to the ways in which the college makes decisions, views the appropriateness of conflict and open disagreement, uses informal more than formal decision-making processes, and is subjected to strong inside or outside constituencies. Language and how it is used are also very important parts of the culture. Using student development jargon in an institution that stresses academic language can jeopardize one's credibility. Moreover, it is important to be able to tell when different aspects of how the institution functions are emerging. While it is convenient to talk about an institution's culture as if it were unidimensional, it is important to be sensitive to the many dimensions and personalities that may emerge. Moreover, while one must be sensitive to the politics of the institution, it is often best not to take on a political demeanor.

Making Sure That There Is a Good Fit. Even in a larger institution, the need to understand and support the nature of its mission, however complex, is very important. In smaller colleges and denominational institutions, the concept of fit is central. Creating opportunities for institutional improvement and change will be very difficult if one is not viewed as essentially in support of or sensitive to the mission. For example, persons who have come out of large public institutions may find themselves having difficulty instituting management improvements. They may be seen as trying to bureaucratize the college. In a denominational college or university, it may be easier for an adherent of the particular denomination or a minister of that denomination to push for fundamental changes than it is for someone who does not belong. The outsider may always be perceived as one. The challenge for a student affairs professional is to distinguish between change that alters the nature of the institution and change that has the potential to improve its effectiveness. One's credibility in the decision-making process will rest on that distinction.

Making the Most of Shared Values. One of the most potent sources of power in creating institutional change is agreement about shared values. While shared values can be used to inhibit change, they can also be used to provide the anchor of agreement around which other changes can be developed. For example, the denominational institution can rely on certain shared values to maintain and enhance community while the institution promotes diversity; thus there is the potential for limiting some of the fragmentation and conflict that occur in a time of fundamental change. In many cases, these special institutions have or can develop sufficiently strong values to facilitate decision making and community building. All too often, these shared values are not used to their potential.

Setting Priorities. Having limited resources and staff requires making sure that priorities are set not only in terms of the student affairs agenda but also in terms of the larger institutional agenda. Using institutional research data and interviews with staff, faculty, and senior administrators can be very helpful and can reinforce the unit's openness to outside influence.

Getting the Most from the Student Affairs Program. A coherent and well-articulated student affairs program will be better understood and supported by the institution than one that is fragmented and not visible. This is a case in which a coherent whole will be much greater than each individual piece. Student affairs professionals in these kinds of institutions often have many more opportunities to speak to faculty, trustees, alumni, and other staff about their work. This is an opportunity that should not be ignored. It will help maintain support and, more important, will encourage others to become involved.

Involving Others. The challenge of limited resources and staff can also be a potential benefit. Student affairs literature constantly calls attention to the need for greater academic and student affairs collaboration. In many institutions, perhaps all, this is too often an uphill battle. Yet in small institutions and denominational colleges, there is greater openness and greater expectation that faculty and others will be involved in the lives of students outside the classroom. It is essential that student affairs support, facilitate, and create opportunities for that involvement. It is also important, however, to be mindful of the fact that the pressures of time that affect student affairs also affect other groups, such as faculty. Their involvement should be meaningful and appropriate.

Getting to Know Others. There are many formal and informal opportunities to be known and to know others. Since the essence of the political process is that different groups bring different perspectives to the decision-making process, knowing others and being known is very important. Open communication creates many opportunities to understand those perspectives and to find creative solutions to differences and conflicts. Taking advantage of these opportunities also means that issues and problems can be anticipated well in advance.

Keeping in Close Touch with Students. In smaller institutions, student affairs professionals are often stretched by playing multiple roles, with many fewer layers of staff support. In this context, ironically, it is sometimes easy to lose touch with students, yet one rich source of power for student affairs is precisely the power that comes from knowing students, working with them to create a positive campus climate, and serving as facilitators in the educational process. For the rest of the institution, this contact, support, and knowledge can position student affairs very powerfully in institutional decision making, which in these kinds of places often concerns matters related to students, such as tuition, curriculum, teaching, enrollment, and retention.

Sensitivity to Timing and Readiness. Larger institutions may be more tolerant of an anarchistic approach to program development, particularly where departments have the staff and resources to initiate something on their own. This is rarely the case in smaller institutions, where new initiatives often involve many others. As a result, it is important to be sensitive to timing and institutional readiness for new programs and ideas. In addition, taking advantage of opportunities can make the difference between very successful administrators and undistinguished ones. For example, when enrollment became one of the major issues on college campuses across the country, student affairs people were presented with a significant opportunity to become central resources to presidents, trustees, and faculty. Those administrators who had collected retention data and who had student satisfaction information and information on those who stayed and withdrew were in a very important position to serve their institutions at a critical time. Some student affairs programs were ready and able to assume leadership; others were not. In small institutions and many religious ones, those who are able to anticipate and respond when the timing is right not only serve student affairs well but also serve their institutions well.

Keeping a Broad Institutional Perspective. For students, faculty, and staff, one of the advantages of being at these very special colleges and universities is the opportunity to see and effect change for the whole institution. This opportunity can be realized only if student affairs professionals are seen as understanding the nature of the institution, its problems, and its challenges. The student affairs role can and should be vital to institutional survival and health. Understanding budget issues, fund raising, enrollment, and retention is essential for almost all student affairs professional staff. It makes the individual more powerful when it comes to reconciling differences or participating in decision making. It also creates an opportunity to position student affairs at the center of institutional decision making.

Accepting Conflict. Ironically, the very same person who may be teaching conflict resolution in a leadership development class for students may be repulsed and passive when it comes to the willingness to participate actively in the genuine conflicts that emerge daily in campuswide decision making. As indicated earlier, the political process is often closely related to adopting a human resources perspective on the institution and on the people with whom one works. In a time of change, conflict may be an undeniable fact of institutional life. For example, campuses that are now making some of the greatest efforts on behalf of achieving a multicultural climate, are the ones experiencing some of the greatest conflicts. Conflict and political struggle are part of creating a pluralistic community. The challenge is to use creative skills to see that conflict and the expression of differences ultimately ensure a stronger community, rather than weakening it.

Conclusion

Colleges and universities can be seen through many lenses—as cultures, human resource communities, anarchies, collegial communities, bureaucracies, and political communities. In fact, they are all of these, in the same way that each individual is a complex combination of the culture in which we live, a reflection of human needs and aspirations, slightly anarchistic or playful, in need of some rules and procedures, collegial, and political. Each of these lenses provides an important perspective on what is occurring. To ignore any one of them, or to assume that only one is accurate, reduces the opportunity to truly understand the dynamics occurring at any particular time. The political activities of the small college and religious institution occur in a unique cultural context and cannot be avoided. Members of these communities have a diversity of perspectives to consider, challenging decisions to make, and limited resources. Student affairs administrators can and must play an essential role in shaping how the political process will unfold in these very special institutions.

References

Astin, A., and Lee, C. *The Invisible Colleges: A Profile of Small, Private Colleges with Limited Resources*. New York: McGraw Hill, 1972.
Baldridge, J. V. *Power and Conflict in the University*. New York: Wiley, 1971.
Barker, R. G., and Gump, P. V. *Big School, Small School*. Stanford, Calif.: Stanford University Press, 1964.
Blau, P. "A Formal Theory of Differentiation in Organizations." *American Sociological Review*, 1970, 35, 201–218.
Block, P. *The Empowered Manager: Positive Political Skills at Work*. San Francisco: Jossey-Bass, 1987.
Boyer, E. *The Condition of the Professoriate: Attitudes and Trends*. Princeton, N.J.: Carnegie Foundation for the Advancement of Teaching, 1989.
Clark, B. "The Organizational Saga in Higher Education." *Administrative Science Quarterly*, 1972, 17 (2), 178–184.
Dahl, R. A. "The Concept of Power." *Behavioral Science*, 1957, 2, 201–215.
Katz, D., and Kahn, R. L. *The Social Psychology of Organizations*. New York: Wiley, 1978.

Pace, R. *The Demise of Diversity?* Princeton, N.J.: Carnegie Commission on Higher Education, 1974.

Pfeffer, J. *Power in Organizations.* Marshfield, Mass.: Pitman Publishing, 1981.

Daryl G. Smith is associate professor of education and psychology, Claremont Graduate School.

Case-study research indicates that the experiences of women and blacks differ significantly from those of their white male counterparts in managing the political dimension of student affairs.

Women and African Americans: Stories Told and Lessons Learned— A Case Study

Helen L. Mamarchev, Mary Lynn Williamson

From a very early age, as a young black male, I learned that paying attention to what was said and left unsaid was important. Being sensitive to nuances and perceptive about subtleties was not just a good idea; it was critical for survival.

There is no doubt in my mind that the fact that I am black has an effect on the political reality of this campus.

When the power brokers on campus pick up the phone and want to talk about a political issue that may be on the table . . . let us just say that I am not the person they think of first.

Political knowledge, a power base, and the ability to successfully work with men were identified by Kuyper (1987) as important factors in the career development of women. In discussing women, blacks, and politics in higher education, three factors immediately become apparent. First, women and blacks are significantly underrepresented at the presidential and vice-presidential levels ("Women and Minority Group Members . . .," 1982). Second, the pressures of working in isolation and in a fishbowl setting may lead practitioners to seriously question the benefits of remaining in leadership roles (Scott and Spooner, 1989). Third, unless those aspiring to leadership positions are provided with the tools they need, they may well find themselves walking through a "revolving door" (Reisser and Zurfluh, 1987).

In an effort to provide information to women and blacks about using political expertise as a tool, a case study was designed and based on three specific research questions: (1) How do women and minorities manage the political dimension of student affairs? (2) Do these administrators manage politics differently from their white male counterparts? (3) Are there barriers that make the effective management of politics more difficult for women and blacks?

Procedure

A literature review of the political dimension of higher education and its relationship to the issues of race and gender yielded little information; however, research on women and blacks in educational administration did offer some applicable insights. Women and African Americans judged to have been successful in managing the political process were identified through exploratory conversations with leaders of professional student affairs associations. A case-study approach was adopted for this inquiry because of a belief that, as Merriam (1988, p. 3) writes, "research focused on discovery, insight, and understanding from the perspectives of those being studied offers the greatest promise of making significant contributions to the knowledge base and practice of education."

Taped conversations, with a formalized interview protocol, were held with thirteen senior-level student affairs administrators. There are six white and seven black administrators in the study. Of the thirteen participants, six are white women, four are black women, and three are black men. Six public colleges or universities, six private institutions, and one public community college, representing all geographical regions of the country, are included. Institutional enrollment ranges from eight hundred to seventy thousand (the latter figure is for a university system).

Limitations of the Study

As in most other qualitative research, the authors make no claims beyond the boundaries of the case study. This information is not intended as representative of all women and all African Americans; however, it is the authors' hope that the power and poignancy of the stories of these exceptional men and women will illuminate the management of institutional politics for all practitioners. In fact, the lessons learned by these individuals are strategies for success that are applicable to all who work in higher education administration.

Recurring Themes

This work represents an effort to synthesize the lessons learned from recent research on women and blacks as it relates to organizational politics, with the stories told by practitioners who have not only survived institutional politics but flourished. Eight major themes identified through this study represent what the participants believe to be the most critical tasks in understanding and managing the political dimension of student affairs. (Quotations that are otherwise unattributed are taken from transcripts of the taped conversations.)

Theme 1: Understand the formal and informal structure of the institution as clearly and completely as possible.

While organizational charts, faculty/staff handbooks, and other written materials provide clear indicators of an institution's formal power structure, identifying the informal structure can be a more exacting task. Regardless of size, however, there does exist in all educational institutions an informal structure. Knowing who the key players in this structure are is crucial if one hopes to effectively manage politics. In writing about upward mobility for women administrators, Stokes (1984) found that 87 percent of the female administrators in her study believed they were excluded from informal networks.

Smith (1985) urges black and white women to find ways to get important data. Identifying the informal power structure is obviously important for gathering such information. Participants in the study offer a number of ways in which the informal structure can be identified. While some methods are more obvious than others, all respondents stress the importance of accurately identifying this organizational configuration:

1. *Observation:* Who eats lunch with whom, who sits next to whom at meetings, and whose families socialize together are small but important signs that may have significance and should not be overlooked.

2. *History:* Pay attention to institutional history. As one administrator said, "Until the late sixties, this institution was all white and all male. That history suggests some political realities that one must be aware of."

3. *Colleagues:* Seek the counsel of colleagues. In the words of another administrator, "Develop strong collegial relationships with others outside your own institution. One way to do this is through active involvement in one or more of the professional associations." Smith (1985) reinforces this concept when she writes that as the rules of the academic game are learned, they must be passed on to female and minority colleagues who will follow.

4. *Acquiring information:* To manage the political dimension effectively, one must have a mind like a computer bank, suggests one respondent: "It has been my experience that, in colleges, incidents, conversations, and developments are rarely unrelated or insignificant. They usually fit together in a larger mosaic. Your job is to put that mosaic together." The ability to take extraneous information and store it for later comparison with other, seemingly unrelated incidents is useful. Effective political managers are able to see the pattern of how these bits of information fit together.

5. *"Gossip":* "One of the things I do upon arrival at a new university is to play my version of the children's game "Gossip," one respondent said. "I start information with one person in the university and wait to see where it ends up, who talked to whom along the way, how long it takes, and what the final content is. That always tells me a lot about the informal structure that I am dealing with."

All participants agree that one should determine as much as possible about the formal and informal structure of an institution during the interview/selection phase prior to accepting a new job. Upon arrival, however, the techniques outlined above should yield a treasure of information critical to the effective management of politics on that campus. As one respondent noted, "If you can learn where the heat is and where the power lies, you will be much better off."

Theme 2: Institutional politics are important. Be prepared to give enormous time, energy, and attention to this aspect of student affairs.

One vice-president observed, "Understanding and managing the political dimension becomes increasingly important as one moves up the organizational ladder." Tinsley (1985) emphasizes the importance of the political dimension in her statement that "the more fully a woman understands her institution's agendas, organizational structures and political processes, the likelier it is that she will achieve."

Separation of oneself from the political dimension is impossible, since there is a political component to virtually everything one does as a chief student affairs officer. Significant percentages of time were reported by all respondents as being spent on politics. Estimates of actual time spent on political activity ranged from 33 to 100 percent. Managing politics is not confined to the vice-presidential level. As one respondent noted, "There is not a unit within student affairs that does not have politics as part of its operational concerns." The importance of politics as part of everyday student affairs work clearly cannot be overlooked, ignored, or taken for granted. In the words of one vice-president,"The political dimension affects virtually everything I do."

Theme 3: Successful management of the political dimension depends primarily on experience, but that experience is different for women and African Americans.

"I do not think there is any way to really learn about politics except through trial and error—hands-on experience," one administrator said. The respondents believe that the experience of women and underrepresented ethnic groups is different from that of their colleagues. They identify three key experiential differences:

1. *Position:* "You begin your professional career knowing that you start out behind your white male friends," said one respondent. Smith (1985,

p. 29) offers a challenge beyond acknowledging one's starting position in the administrative race, by exhorting black and white women to move beyond sexism and racism by observing "whatever occupies our minds, motivates our behavior."

2. *Perception:* The female and black experiences mean sensitivity to and perception about nuances and subtleties: "It means reading between the lines, listening for what is left unsaid, and not taking anything for granted."

3. *Preparation:* In addition to obtaining the appropriate credentials and time-in-line experience (Ost and Twale, 1989), our respondents and other writers (Smith, 1985) stress learning how to recognize sources of power and befriending those in positions of power.

Graduate programs are seen as woefully inadequate in their training for the political dimension. Only one participant reported that her Ph.D. program actually helped prepare her for the reality of institutional politics.

The poor or less successful examples of others are cited as a major component of the participants' political education: "I learned how to successfully manage politics by watching those around me and then doing things differently than they did." Since the experience of women and African Americans is markedly different from that of their white male colleagues, since preparation programs do not prepare their graduates for political life in higher education, and since professionals frequently see poor models, it becomes increasingly clear why so many practitioners rely on trial and error. The participants in this study are all successful managers of the political domain; however, one cannot help questioning the wisdom of such a haphazard approach to training the profession's leadership.

Because of these problems of preparation and education, simply recruiting women or blacks into the profession does not guarantee that those individuals will reach senior administrative levels. As Oberst (1987, p. 4) aptly states, "The idealistic notion of a pipeline implies that if we increase the number of women and minorities at the entry level, they will automatically and inevitably work their way through until they eventually emerge at the top. . . . But, when we look at the careers of people who have been in that pipeline for a decade, we begin to suspect that the pipeline needs to be checked frequently and ought to be equipped with strategically placed pumping stations along the way, if anything is to come out the other end."

The respondents identified several "pumping stations along the way," which hold significant potential for improving the experience of and thus the opportunity for women and blacks to be successful political managers. Ph.D. programs need to include coursework on the political process and its effective management. Staff development programs on individual campuses and in professional conferences need to focus on this topic. Summer institutes, with politics as a central focus, could be developed and offered by the professional asssociations. Such workshops and training opportunities would serve as excellent opportunities for women and blacks who are aspiring chief student affairs officers. The attitude should be, in the words of one of the respondents, that "politics is not a four-letter word."

Theme 4: Women and African Americans manage the politics of an institution differently from their white male counterparts.

"I do not believe that there is anything inherent in one's gender or ethnicity which makes it more or less difficult to manage politics. There are, however, some things about the ways in which women and minorities are socialized that are barriers," observed one respondent. Stokes (1984) has written of the organizational barriers and their impact on women in higher education. Davis and Watson (1982, p. 2) discuss cultural barriers for blacks in this way: "We often find ourselves in foreign social space, [with] unfamiliar protocol, habits, manners, values, and style[s] of thinking that are new." The following techniques for overcoming barriers were reported by all participants:

1. *Compromise:* Respondents reported that they were willing to compromise more frequently than their white male colleagues were on a wide range of issues.

2. *Initiating contact:* Being the first to reach out, pick up the phone, or ask someone to lunch is a recurring theme.

3. *Resisting turfism:* Resisting this impulse and thinking of the whole institution, instead of one's territory, are frequently mentioned.

4. *Battle selection:* "I choose my battles wisely. I do not react to every little thing."

5. *Humor:* Participants use humor to confront: "A sense of humor and the ability to play in an organization is important at the executive level, because it is so unexpected."

6. *Confronting expectations:* Often women and blacks are perceived as being there to serve only one constituency. One vice-president spoke convincingly about this issue: "How does one compensate if race is an issue? Demonstrate competence and remain confident that others will recognize that competence. Confront the expectation that one works only with black students or female students. Teach others that you are there to serve all students."

Every black administrator in the study reported that he or she felt excluded from informal, social gatherings at his or her institution, to some degree. Many identified such social events as important parts of the informal power structure. One noted, "As the vice-president for student affairs, I am invited to all the formal university social activities. However, there are numerous informal social gatherings to which I am not invited. That becomes evident at Monday morning staff meetings." Interestingly, none of the white females interviewed mentioned similar exclusion at all.

A second difference between white females and black respondents, both male and female, was found in the ways in which the black respondents compensated for their exclusion from certain campus social activities. The community surrounding the campus, regardless of campus size, became the place where blacks effectively compensated. The Rotary, Kiwanis, and Lions clubs, as well as United Way, local arts and theatre, and churches, were given as examples of community involvement. Visible leadership in such activities was seen as improving one's value on campus. One respondent noted, "As blacks, we have to utilize everything available to us in order to compensate for opportunities, groups, and social outlets that are closed off."

Theme 5: Teaching younger professionals about politics assumes greater importance for chief student affairs officers who are women or African Americans.
"I never had a real mentor. That is why it is so important for me to mentor young professionals," stated one vice-president. Moore (1982) identifies mentoring, either formal or informal, as important for women but notes that only one-fourth to one-third of college administrators have had mentors. Mentoring, for these respondents, was clearly a conscious decision. Almost all reported mentoring in formalized ways, in which the political dimension of student affairs was discussed.

Networking was also identified by the participants as an item to be discussed with younger professionals. According to the study respondents, networking was particularly important for blacks. "One of the things about being black in a white world is that we have always had a network about communicating political realities. This is an unspoken but nevertheless real effort to communicate with one another about the political reality of dealing with a majority world."

Visibility to one's staff, the faculty, students, and other administrators is a key factor in teaching young professionals. The value of "management by walking around," or MBWA, was popularized by Peters and Waterman (1982). Respondents who employ this management tool in their own student affairs divisions reported that the increased visibility has proved its worth. A perception of "approachability" is established. In addition, being present, particularly in times of crisis, enables the chief student affairs officer to evaluate the performance of staff. This on-site appraisal offers excellent opportunities for specific advice, as well as encouragement. While a number of vice-presidents reported using this technique, it could more properly be abbreviated as TBWA, or "teaching by walking around." After all, as one vice-president described it, "I am not just in the management business. I am in the teaching business. One of the things we have an obligation to teach about is politics."

Modeling was also frequently mentioned as a way to teach about politics. All respondents stated that they either see themselves as role models or feel that others view them in that light. They clearly understand that it is their effectiveness in their jobs that helps open doors for others who are rising through the organization: "The best thing I can do for women at my university is to be an effective vice-president. If I deliver, I am perceived as being effective and am effective; that cannot hurt women."

Theme 6: Those who successfully manage the political dimension of student affairs attribute much of their success to their feelings of positive self-worth.

"I have never believed that people could ever do anything better than I could simply because they were men or members of another race. That belief has made all the difference." This remark summarizes a dominant thread running through all the interviews. Reviewing the literature on women in education, Goerss (1977) suggests that women administrators possess very strong self-images. Evans's (1986) research on the self-concept of women in student affairs administration indicates that the women interviewed for her study also exhibited strong, positive self-concepts.

All the participants in the study reported some minor decisions that they would make differently if given the opportunity to repeat their careers. Those without the Ph.D. noted that they would obtain that credential; others said that they would work harder at developing their "cocktail party" skills and that they would seek out the "right people" for lunch more often. Several people mentioned that they would have attuned themselves to political agendas earlier in their careers. None, however, reported that any of these things really matter, since "if you like the person you are today, then all those past experiences, even the mistakes, made you that way."

Self-esteem is the one thing that truly does matter, according to these successful vice-presidents. They repeatedly emphasized the necessity for this trait, coupled with the valuable skills of precise communication, active listening, clarity of thought, careful analysis, and highly honed problem-solving. These were not seen as political skills or executive skills but rather as simply those needed for effective living. Self-esteem, however, was a dominant finding of this study and cannot be overemphasized: "People treat you the way you treat yourself."

Theme 7: Successful management of the political dimension requires a clearly articulated set of ethical standards, which cannot be compromised, regardless of the politics of the situation.

"You really need a strong sense of self and ethics, and you cannot have any obvious chinks in your armor." Ethical principles were directly or indirectly referred to in over fifty instances during the thirteen interviews. Among women and blacks, any deviation from one's personal code was viewed as a chink in the armor and therefore a problem. It is impossible to believe, however, that these individuals implement an ethical code in their daily lives simply to avoid the liability of such "chinks." Both the frequency with which ethics was discussed and the conviction demonstrated in conversation after conversation lead to the inescapable conclusion that this is not simply a "flavor of the month" topic; enduring ethical standards were viewed as important guiding principles, which directly affect how one manages politics.

Stability, solidity, and the appearance of always being in control of situations seemed to be very important for women and African Americans. To appear otherwise suggests weakness and indecision, which may lead to ineffectiveness, according to this group. In short, they must always be on guard. Whether this expectation is imposed by oneself or by others was unclear; however, that expectation was a reality for these individuals. One observed, "My male counterparts are always looking for women and minorities to fail."

The notion of personal/institutional fit was used numerous times in discussing ethics. Not only must one have clearly articulated ethical principles and employ them in the everyday performance of one's job, but successful chief student affairs officers also said it was important to find an institution that reflects values similar to one's own. Institutional values are pervasive throughout the formal and informal structures, manifesting themselves in action and policy decisions. Ascertaining what values the institution holds, and analyzing one's own fit with those values, are crucial steps that come before accepting a new position. One vice-president declared, "I have a set of standards that I try to live by. How well the institution reflects those values is an important consideration. One can never violate those standards." In a study designed to assess factors that women administrators identified as contributing to their desire to resign from leadership roles, Reisser and Zurfluh's (1987) findings reinforce the notion of gaps between personal and institutional values.

Theme 8: Incorporating the language of sports and war into everyday conversation is critical for chief student affairs officers who are women or African Americans.

"The combination of military structure with team sport operation is a natural one from management's point of view" (Harragan, 1977, p. 67). The language of almost all those interviewed for this study reasonates with vivid sports and military metaphors. Participants described success in the political dimension as dependent on understanding the rules of the game, the team concept, and the strategies of war. Phrases used most frequently included "damn the battleships," "choose your battles wisely," "be part of the team," "get to know the referees," "know all the players," and "quickly learn what the rules of the game are." Cummings (1979) suggests that new kinds of training programs should be designed for women to develop an understanding of the male paradigms—specifically, sports and military metaphors—that shape work relations. These are examples from the respondents. "You cannot play successfully if you are using amateur rules and everyone else is using professional rules." "People will give you things to do that you could fumble. If you hold on and work hard, however, you might score a touchdown, and then people will look at you differently." Ernst (1982) supports this notion by arguing that women, given a sufficient probability of success, should accept tasks and appointments in areas where they have limited background.

Playing the game at one's institution is extremely important for success in managing politics. Pearson, Shavlik, and Touchton (1989) say that, since the 1970s, women and African Americans are being taken more seriously in higher education and some changes have occurred. They also argue, however, that institutions of higher education are basically unchanged at the core. Leadership by white males and instruction by white males still dominate, as does a value system for establishing priorities and making hard decisions that does not include the agendas of women and blacks. They conclude that because women and blacks continue to be evaluated by white male norms, higher education still does not fully reflect the richness of the life experiences of these groups.

Winning at institutional politics, according to these chief student affairs officers, is contingent on completely understanding the rules of the game. Further, they acknowledged that these rules must be followed if one is to be credible within the academy. Several participants talked about being the sole exception in a white male culture filled with shared experiences that make game playing easy and natural: "In a room full of males, there is a tacit, shared sense of what is going on. That male bonding thing is real and very strong. Whenever there is a lull in the conversation, they start talking about sports. That shared sense of sports carries over to how they do business as grownups. It is difficult to describe, but it is real." The key to success for these repondents seems to lie in their ability to display behaviors deemed acceptable by their counterparts, and that also allow them to contribute to the university in significant ways.

Strategies for Survival

Critical for success is the ability to survive all the games and maneuvers occurring in the political environment. All respondents acknowledged that, over time, they had used certain behaviors or responses to survive continuing challenges to their credibility and performance. The following comments reflect general suggestions that should be incorporated by those who aspire to be chief student affairs officers:

> Realize that male colleagues are colleagues, and working with them is what this is all about.

Keep track of whom you owe, who owes you, and when to call in favors.

Work harder than anyone else. You have heard the phrase "work smarter, not harder." As blacks and women, we must work harder *and* smarter.

Be competent. There is no substitute.

Never forget to whom you report.

Do not cross people without a reason.

Reach out to help those who need it, both professionally and personally. People will remember that in tough times.

Give meaningful praise and credit.

Be honest and straightforward. Convince others that there is no hidden agenda in student affairs.

Be open, and do not attempt to hide problems. If problems are out in the open, people have less to shoot at.

Recognize that others' perceptions of you, simply because of race and gender, cannot be ignored. They must be acknowledged, understood, and confronted.

Attend small social events where others do not expect you. Retirement parties for custodial workers are a good example. By doing so, you gain credibility, not only for yourself but for your division.

Do not be afraid to open yourself up to possible mentors of all races and either gender.

Develop a specific area of expertise. This will increase both visibility and credibility with faculty and other administrators.

Just hang on. The longer you last at an institution, the less race or gender becomes an issue.

Are politics important? According to these respondents, the answer is a resounding yes: "No matter how competent you are, no matter how much you believe in yourself, no matter how much integrity you may have, if you do not understand the politics of your institution, you will not last."

Conclusion

The themes identified in this chapter are the stories told and lessons learned of an exceptionally capable group of women and African Americans. As a final note, these people love what they do. They are all tremendously enthusiastic about student affairs work, despite having to overcome significant barriers because of race and gender. It is the authors' hope that we have done justice to the vibrancy and vision of their ideas:

> I enjoy the gamesmanship. I often feel as if I am marching to a different beat from the drummer, but I do not know if that is because I am younger, I am black, I am female, or just me. I do not like labels. Try to put me in a box or a category, and you are in trouble. I am just me, and the folks here are learning to deal with me—not expectations or stereotypes—just me.

References

Cummings, N. P. "Women in Educational Administration." In M. Berry (ed.), *Women in Educational Administration.* Washington, D.C.: National Association for Women Deans, Administrators, and Counselors, 1979.

Davis, G., and Watson, G. *Black Life in Corporate America.* Garden City, N.J.: Anchor Press, 1982.

Ernst, R. J. "Women in Higher Education Leadership Positions—It Doesn't Happen by Accident." *Journal of the College and University Personnel Association,* 1982, *33* (2), 19–22.

Evans, N. J. "The Self-Concept of Women in Educational and Student Affairs Administration." *Journal of NAWDAC,* 1986, *50* (1), 14–19.

Goerss, K.V.W. *Women Administrators in Education: A Review of Research, 1960–1976.* Ruth Strang Research Award Monograph Series, no. 3. Washington, D.C.: National Association for Women Deans, Administrators, and Counselors, 1977.

Harragan, B. L. *Games Mother Never Taught You: Corporate Gamesmanship for Women.* New York: Warner Books, 1977.

Kuyper, L. A. "Career Development of Women in the Administration of Higher Education: Contributing Factors." *Journal of NAWDAC,* 1987, *50* (4), 3–7.

Merriam, S. B. *Case Study Research in Education: A Qualitative Approach.* San Francisco: Jossey-Bass, 1988.

Moore, K. M. "The Role of Mentors in Developing Leaders for Academe." *Educational Record,* 1982, *63,* 23–28.

Oberst, B. *Assessing Change: A Profile of Women and Minorities in Higher Education Administration at State and Land-Grant Universities.* Washington, D.C.: National Association of State Universities and Land-Grant Colleges, 1987.

Ost, D. H., and Twale, D. J. "Appointments of Administrators in Higher Education: Reflections of Administrative and Organizational Structures." In *Initiatives of NAWDAC.* Washington, D.C.: National Association for Women Deans, Administrators, and Counselors, 1989.

Pearson, C. S., Shavlik, D. L., and Touchton, J. G. *Educating the Majority: Women Challenge Tradition in Higher Education.* New York: Macmillan, 1989.

Peters, T. J., and Waterman, R. A., Jr. *In Search of Excellence: Lessons from America's Best-Run Companies.* New York: Warner Books, 1982.

Reisser, L. J., and Zurfluh, L. A. "Female Administrators: Moving Up or Moving Out?" *Journal of NAWDAC,* 1987, *50* (4), 22–29.

Scott, N A., and Spooner, S. "Women Administrators: Stressors and Strategies." In *Initiatives of NAWDAC.* Washington, D.C.: National Association for Women Deans, Administrators, and Counselors, 1989.

Smith, E. "Upward Mobility: Black and White Women Administrators." *Journal of NAWDAC,* 1985, *48* (3), 28–32.

Stokes, M. J. *Organizational Barriers and Their Impact on Women in Higher Education.* Report no. HE-018-644. Washington, D.C.: National Association for Women Deans, Administrators, and Counselors, 1984.

Tinsley, A. "Upward Mobility for Women Administrators." *Journal of NAWDAC,* 1985, *49* (1), 3–11.

"Women and Minority-Group Members in Administrative Posts." *Chronicle of Higher Education,* Feb. 3, 1982, p. 4.

Helen Marmachev is associate vice-president for student affairs at the University of Florida.

Mary Lynn Williamson is assistant vice-president for student affairs, SUNY College, Old Westbury, New York.

.

This chapter presents a model within which to view the potential conflict between the political (doing things right) and the ethical (doing the right thing).

Ethical Issues and Administrative Politics

M. Lee Upcraft, Thomas G. Poole

The authors of the preceding chapters in this volume have done an excellent job of providing political strategies for getting things done and getting them done right. However, there is or at least there should be some consideration of whether, when doing things right, one also considers doing the right thing. Put another way, what are the ethical implications of being politically astute? In this chapter, we will review ethical implications of administrative decisions. We will present several cases to illustrate the potential conflict between the political (doing things right) and the ethical (doing the right thing). Finally, we will present a model that helps the administrator identify the extent to which administrative dilemmas impinge on moral considerations.

Ethical Issues and Administrative Politics: Some Dilemmas

There are many instances in the life of a student affairs administrator when being political may be in conflict with being ethical. It is not that the two are necessarily incompatible or that all administrative dilemmas are necessarily ethical dilemmas, but there are times when the political has implications for the ethical and the ethical may have implications for the political. Take the following cases, for example.

The contemporary language of organizational theory would substitute the terms *transactional leadership* and *transformative leadership* for the terms *management* and *leadership*.

Hiring Dilemmas. You may be torn between hiring two equally qualified candidates for a job in your organization. One candidate is an experienced professional, with excellent credentials and positive recommendations. In his interview, he came across very well but seemed to lack enthusiasm. The second candidate is a much less experienced professional, also with positive recommendations. In his interview, he came across as a very enthusiastic and high-energy person. Whom would you hire, and why?

Using this same example, let us further assume that your organization has no African American professionals. What if you decide that the first candidate is most qualified? He is white. The second candidate, also qualified, is African American. Whom do you hire? You may be torn between your commitment to hire the best candidate, on the one hand, and your commitment to affirmative action, on the other. How do you decide between two very importantly held but competing values? Is there a politically correct decision?

Personal and Institutional Values. A second example, posed by Brown in Chapter Two of this volume, concerns what you do after you have had your say and your point of view is not accepted. Brown suggests that you have three choices: support the decision, say nothing, or resign. Suppose the decision is that your institution will continue to hold its investments in companies doing business in South Africa. Further, suppose that you have been active in your church's efforts to support divestment.

It certainly would be expedient to hold your tongue and support the decision not to divest. Further, it may be sound politics in that your ability to influence future decisions may rest with your compliance in this case. But is it ethical to support a decision with which you disagree, especially if that decision violates an importantly held value? How do you decide?

A conflict between your values and those of your institution is not the only type of ethical dilemma you encounter as an administrator. There are times when you may be faced with deciding between the best interests of an individual and the general welfare of all members of the collegiate community.

Confidentiality and the Common Good. Suppose that your policy on sexual assault clearly states that the confidentiality of the victim will be maintained. A rape victim is treated at your health service and is clearly mentally distressed. She refuses to give any information about the circumstances of her sexual assault and just wants to be left alone. Let us also suppose this is the fourth "stranger rape" on your campus in the last two weeks. On the one hand, you believe the rights of the victim must be respected; on the other hand, failure to get more information about this assault could endanger the lives of other women.

When this rape is unlikely to come to the public's attention, the political solution might be not to press the matter and to hope that there are no more rapes. But would you feel ethically responsible if another rape occurred that you might have prevented had you pursued the matter more vigorously with the victim? How do you decide? **Competing Interests.** Another type of ethical dilemma may arise when you have to choose the best interests of one group over those of another. Suppose your institution has proposed a two-year tuition freeze in order to sustain enrollments. But that also means a salary freeze for your very hardworking and productive staff. If you do not support the freeze, you know that many students will be forced to drop out or transfer. If you do support the freeze, chances are that some of your high-performing staff will suffer economic hardship or leave for better pay. You are torn by your responsibility to advocate both for the best interests of your students and for the best interests of your staff. Either way, some people you care about will be adversely affected.

The political solution might be to support the freeze, because public opinion is strongly supportive of keeping costs down and you would be supportive of an institutional position. However, the ethical solution might be to continue to fight against the freeze, advocating on behalf of your staff, because without them, students will inevitably suffer. How do you decide?

There are undoubtedly many other examples of dilemmas where the political and the ethical conflict. The question then becomes the basis on which to resolve this potential conflict. One answer may be that you deal with situations one at a time and make decisions consistent with each situation. Sometimes that would mean being political and sometimes ethical. The problem with this situational solution is that you may create precedents in one situation that may bind you in another. It may also label you as one who has no consistent ethical principles—that is, unless there is some underlying conceptual framework within which each situation can be addressed.

Existing Models of Decision Making

Some such underlying frameworks already exist. For example, many student affairs professional associations have issued general codes of conduct for the practitioners in their respective areas. In the case of the National Association of Student Personnel Administrators (NASPA), for instance, standards of professional practice were developed in 1983, to foster certain values: "personal integrity, belief in the dignity and worth of individuals, respect for individual differences, a commitment to service, and dedication to the development of individuals through education and personal growth" (Canon and Brown, 1985, p. 99). The standards also target several areas of administrative responsibility in which ethical dilemmas may arise. These include caveats regarding conflicts of interest, legal authority, nondiscrimination, confidentiality of records, performance evaluations, and a number of others (Canon and Brown, 1985).

In a similar fashion, the ethical principles and standards of the American College Personnel Association (ACPA) outline general ethical advice that relates to four primary constituencies—the profession, the student, the institution, and society. In the area of professional responsibility, for example, ACPA members are urged to "adopt a professional lifestyle characterized by [the] use of sound theoretical principles and a personal value system congruent with the basic tenets of the profession" (American College Personnel Association, 1990, p. 199). The standards also address specific areas of potential conflict, such as sexual harassment, limits of confidentiality, conduct of research, and many others.

Ethical codes such as these help to outline the boundaries of acceptable professional behavior. They remind us to be good people and responsible professionals and indicate some ways in which we can achieve those goals. However, professional codes of conduct give very little guidance for the solving of the value conflicts just described. Rather than helping us to answer our questions about moral conduct, they help us to raise more questions. If, as the NASPA standards suggest, we are to "demonstrate and promote responsible behavior for students" (Canon and Brown, 1985, p. 100), what do we define as responsible? Is this behavior equally responsible in all situations? The ACPA statement recommends that we refrain from "imping[ing] on colleagues' dignity, moral code, privacy, worth, professional functioning, and/or personal growth" (American College Personnel Association, 1990, p. 199). But what are the attitudes and actions that impinge? Further, is it never my obligation to impinge on my colleagues' moral code?

Professional codes, by their very nature, are unable to provide the answers to the moral dilemmas in which we find ourselves as student affairs professionals. This is why the ACPA has augmented its statement with the five ethical principles that have resulted from the pioneering work of Karen Strohm Kitchener, who has devised a model for moral decision making in student affairs.

Kitchener's model presents a two-tiered system of ethical justification. The first level is intuition. Borrowing from Hare (see Kitchener, 1984), she notes that moral intuition leads people to "an immediate, prereflective response to most ethical situations based on the sum of their prior ethical knowledge and experience" (Kitchner, 1984, p. 44). These immediate moral feelings are critical for resolving routine ethical dilemmas, but they are not sufficient, for they "cannot always be trusted to lead to good ethical decisions" (Kitchner, 1984, p. 44). The critical-evaluative level of moral reasoning is necessary, in order to refine and evaluate our judgments. Here, Kitchener suggests a hierarchy of moral guidelines that is increasingly general and abstract. It begins with ethical rules, (for example, professional codes and laws), progresses to ethical principles, and culminates with ethical theories.

One of the strengths of Kitchener's model is its recognition of the inadequacy of professional codes in helping us to resolve our most serious moral problems. For times when these ethical rules fall short, Kitchener recommends five ethical principles that may be considered binding: autonomy, beneficence, nonmaleficence, justice, and fidelity. If these, too, fail to shed light, one moves to the highest level of moral reasoning—ethical theory—where one is to decide for a universalizable or generalizable course of action (Kitchener, 1985).

Kitchener's model, while advancing moral discourse in the student affairs profession, stops short of helping to decipher many administrative dilemmas that pit the political against the ethical. The reason for this is to be found in the resources to which Kitchener looked for the identification of her ethical principles. Kitchener's model borrows the ethical principles that are central to biomedical ethics, especially as these have been outlined by Beauchamp and Childress (1989), and Ramsey (1970). In the health care setting, such notions as autonomy, beneficence, nonmaleficence, justice, and fidelity serve to set the moral tone for the relationship between doctor and patient, although the principle of justice deals with social policy—that is, the guaranteed availability of minimal health care (Beauchamp and Childress, 1989).

The practitioner-patient dynamic readily lends itself to the counseling facets of the student services profession but may not offer much help in other areas. For example, the principle of autonomy—the ability of the patient or client to make a free, informed, rational decision about treatment options—is at the core of medical ethics. One's degree of autonomy must be ascertained in order to justify both the giving and the withholding of care. Such is also the case in counseling relationships. In other areas of student affairs, however, autonomy is not always a decisive issue. With increasing frequency, it is erroneously interjected into campus debates over certain rights—the right of free speech, the right to privacy and confidentiality, and so on. But this shifts the focus from the condition of the actor, as a moral agent, to legal protections that pertain to all persons, regardless of their moral autonomy. In other words, autonomy relates to one's mental and intellectual ability to make a decision, rather than to the removal of legal and physical restraints on certain behaviors. The First Amendment right to free speech does not begin to address the degree of moral autonomy possessed by the speaker.

To give further consideration to the shortcomings of Kitchener's model, let us consider the following case. The student government president, who has been pressuring the institution's administration for an open budget, stops by to see a trusted student affairs staff member. Upon entering the room, he says, "I need to talk privately with you. I'm in a bit of a bind, and I need some advice. Can we talk confidentially?" The staff member agrees, assuming that they are about to discuss some aspect of the student's personal life. The student proceeds to explain how, while he was sitting at his desk, a plain brown wrapper was slid under his door. He unwrapped it to find a copy of last year's salaries of all the central administrators, information that had never seen the light of day but could now provide a powerful weapon in the fight for an open budget. The student clearly identifies his moral dilemma: What do I do with these figures? What he may not realize is that he has also created a moral dilemma for the staff member. Does she break confidentiality and share what she knows with her superiors? The staff member's dilemma is intensified when the student, realizing that he is speaking to a student activist of a former generation, goes on to ask, "What would you do if you were in my position?"

In this case, the concept of autonomy does not help to clarify a response. The staff member is a free moral agent, as is the student. In fact, we can go through the entire list of ethical principles that Kitchener suggests and gain very little insight. What does it mean to do no harm in this context? No harm to whom—the student, the university, the staff member's career? To do good? What is the good in this situation? Are there competing goods? To do justice? Again, we are left to wonder what is just in this case. To be loyal? To whom, the staff member asks—my employer, my boss, or the covenant of confidentiality I made with this student? Here, we see that the values of the biomedical model are not universally applicable.

Kitchener would then advise us to utilize an ethical theory, such as the utilitarian obligation to do the greatest good for the greatest number. But what is the greatest good? If we were to apply Kitchener's model to each of the administrative dilemmas posed at the outset of this chapter, we might very well arrive at a similar state of confusion.

Understanding Our Moral Dilemmas

The cases presented at the beginning of this chapter help us to see that we must learn to identify the nature of our moral dilemmas before we can solve them. In many of the hypothetical cases, two potential conflicts were present: between our individual values and those of our institution, and between the professional expectations for sound administration and moral leadership. Some administrators might not see the conflicts at all. For these people, institutional policy might be construed as fully trustworthy; no conflict of conscience can arise by following policy. Other people might feel caught in a moral thicket by every administrative challenge or institutional expectation. The majority of administrators probably fall somewhere in between these extremes. Nonetheless, one cannot begin to solve a moral dilemma without accurately identifying it.

This point is supported by the research of Rest (1986), who identified the major components of moral reasoning in young adults. These components, which seem to hold true generally, are identifying the moral dimension of the situation, defining the ideal moral choice, deciding on a course of action, and acting as a moral agent. It is Rest's first component, identification of the moral dilemma, that sets the tone for our moral agency. Failing to see the moral dimension of a situation, or inaccurately assessing the moral dimension, will lead inevitably to moral confusion.

The primacy of correctly interpreting the situation leads us to another conceptual framework for thinking about ethics in student affairs. We are not suggesting this as a model of decision making, nor are we claiming that this framework solves any problems. Rather, it is designed to conceptualize the facets of professional and personal responsibilities in a way that can aid our identification of moral conflicts in the administrative arena.

The axes of the grid in Figure 1 are provided by two distinct but related fields of tension often encountered in administrative moral dilemmas. The first is the tension between the individual (the moral agent) and the community or communities in which we live and to which we relate. These include other individuals, the institution, professional organizations, and others. This axis represents that polarity between the moral agent, with his or her personal values, and the values of the community or communities. These sometimes conflict.

Along an intersecting axis lies the tension between two professional expectations of student services administrators—management and leadership. Much of the ethical confusion in higher education (and in the business sector) can be blamed on the inability of some individuals to distinguish between these two areas. In many cases, the moral has been reduced to good management. The distinction between management and leadership is an important one, for the ethical component is the differen-

Figure 1. Conceptual Framework for Ethics

MANAGEMENT

Skills (1)	Obligations (2)
Time management	Policies
Conflict resolution	Strategic plans
Listening skills	Job descriptions
Goal setting	Unit goals
	Professional Codes

INDIVIDUAL ———————————————— COMMUNITY

Virtues (3)	Values (4)
Courage	Justice
Moderation	Openness
Prudence	Discipline
Responsibility	Caring

LEADERSHIP

tiating factor. As the late A. Bartlett Giamatti once instructed the administrators at Yale, "Management is the capacity to handle multiple problems, neutralize various constituencies, motivate personnel. . . . Leadership, on the other hand, is an essentially moral act, not—as in most management— an essentially protective act. It is the assertion of a vision, not simply the exercise of a style" (Cited in Deford, 1989, p. 88).

The first quadrant locates those personal skills that one must possess to be a good administrator. These include such traits as time management, goal setting, organizing skills, conflict resolution, and so on. Without these qualities, the ability to manage effectively is hampered. At the same time, these are not moral categories; that is, if I do not manage my time wisely, I might be an ineffective administrator but not necessarily an evil person. The second quadrant defines one's relationships as a professional to a number of communities. These relationships can be characterized and evaluated according to mutually recognized obligations and agreements, such as job descriptions, unit goals, strategic plans, policies, and professional codes. The third quadrant identifies the personal virtues that the professional, as a human being, brings to the moral task of leadership. This includes what Kitchener (1984, 1985) calls our ordinary moral sense. Formal schools of ethics might refer to this as one's conscience or character. In either case, we are pointing to those personal values that are evident in the sort of person we have become. In the fourth quadrant, we have replaced Kitchener's ethical principles with those that Boyer (1990) cites.

The personal virtues can be defined briefly. Courage is necessary for the public display of moral leadership. The courageous person is not fearless but fears what is natural for us to fear; that is, the courageous person fears the right things, for the right reason, and faces them in the right way (Aristotle, 1977). Such fortitude includes an unwillingness to compromise one's principles, enduring public ridicule and "the loneliness of being misunderstood" (Browne, 1967, p. 46).

Moderation, or temperance, relates to self-control. It is the capacity to stand up to others, rather than being dominated by them. At the same time, it means not thinking more highly of oneself than one ought to think. In addition, moderation implies a sense of discrimination, which enables one to decide from among a number of issues, picking and choosing which battles are worth fighting and which are not.

According to the ancient philosophers and theologians, prudence refers to the practical wisdom that comes with maturity and reflection on life's experiences. This is the quality that helps us to see beyond the merely visible, to hear beyond the audible, so that we can identify and understand the underlying meaning of events and their connections. Prudence governs our exercise of all the other virtues by helping us know, not whether truth telling, for example, is right, but when the truth is to be spoken and how. Hauerwas (1980) tells a story from his own life that illustrates the need for this practical wisdom. Hauerwas was raised in a Western home by hardworking parents. His father, a laborer and craftsman, seldom expressed his affection for his children; it was simply assumed to be the basis of his providing for the family. Such provision included giving the children the opportunity to go to college. When Hauerwas finished college and enrolled in Yale Divinity School, he was beginning to see that he was becoming more and more unlike his parents. Higher education had given him the opportunity to experience things they would never know—art and music, diverse kinds of people, new understandings of religion, and so on. During Hauerwas's second year in divinity school, his father began to build a deer rifle. Every time Stanley called home, the primary news was about his father's progress on the gun. That summer, Hauerwas and his wife headed out West for a visit with his parents. As he entered the door, his father proudly thrust the completed rifle into his hands. It was a beautiful piece of work, but Hauerwas, responding out of his convictions about truth telling and the nation's gun policy, said, "Of course you realize that it will not be long before we as a society are going to have to take all these things away from you people" (Hauerwas, 1980, p. 463). Looking back on that incident, Hauerwas still regards his statement as reflecting a sound social policy. In that sense, it was true. Yet he now sees that to have made such a remark in that context was a moral failure of the first order. The nature of the shortcoming did not involve lack of formal training in ethics, nor was it concerned with the absence of a model for decision making. As he put it, "the failure of my response to my father . . . showed that *I did not yet have sufficient character to provide me with the moral skills to know that I had been given a gift and how to respond appropriately*" (Hauerwas, 1980, p. 464; italics in original). In other words, Hauerwas's comment reflected a lack of prudence, the deep understanding of what was taking place beneath the observable events. A prudent person would have seen the gift of love and pride, not the gun.

The fourth virtue is responsibility. In classical ethical theory, this notion focused, quite literally, on the ability of the moral agent to respond. It raised the question of degrees of freedom against levels of determinism. In contemporary ethics, responsibility is thought of in broader terms. It includes the relational aspects of moral agency. The responsible person asks, "What is the situation in which I am asked to respond? Who are the other actors, and how has their response affected me?" Niebuhr (1963) points out that the responsible person poses a complex series of moral questions, unlike people who are simply driven by laws, rules, policies, goals, or what we might call "the bottom line." Those whose actions are governed by laws, rules, and policies ask, "What is right according to the highest law?" Those who strive for the highest good ask, "What is the way to achieve the desired outcome?" The former is concerned with the right, no matter what may happen to the good, while the latter subordinates the right to the highest good.

However, the responsible self must first ask the prudent question "What is going on here?" This represents the attempt to both define the situation and identify the moral conflict in it. Once this is achieved, one can pose the moral question "What is fitting?" The responsible self is not merely a free moral agent but rather a conscious interpreter of human interaction. Further, the responsible moral agent is accountable. Responsibility lies in that person who stays with, who owns, his or her action. Responsibility lies in that agent who recognizes that there will be consequences for action, most of which will be in the form of responses from other responsible selves. Thus the pattern of responsibility, according to Niebuhr (1963, p. 65) includes "the idea of an agent's action as response to an action upon him in accordance with his interpretation of the latter action and with his expectation of response to his response; and all of this is in a continuing community of agents." All of this is to say that, along with the necessity to choose, come the consequences of one's choice. The pragmatic notion of prudence and the multiple considerations made by Niebuhr's responsible self resonate with the multidimensional dilemmas in which many student affairs administrators find themselves.

Community values, as described by Boyer (1990, p. 3), pertain to what he describes as a "purposeful community"—namely, the college or university "where the intellectual life is central and where faculty and students work together to strengthen teaching and learning on the campus." In this setting, certain values are needed to regulate community life. The first of these is justice.

By *justice*, we mean not only the fair distribution of goods, powers, and opportunities but also the retributive concern for redress of historical wrongs and grievances. This latter aspect is an essential element of the moral discourse of higher education. On our campuses, we are dealing with such issues as racism, homophobia, sexism, and anti-Semitism. In discussing these issues, many students and faculty members in the majority populations often assume that everyone is playing on an even playing field, where merit and achievement alone are honored. Justice, from this perspective, is often defined as that which feels fair to oneself. Justice is related to fairness when it means the redress of historic grievances; it is not, however, the same as equality. As Browne (1967, p. 46) has observed, to be just means to treat "each individual differently and all as human."

The second communal value is *openness*. For Boyer (1990), this notion includes both uncompromised protection of freedom of expression and clear preference for honest and civil discourse. Speech must not be regulated for any reason, he argues, but when boundaries of honesty and decency have been crossed, the community must denounce the violation "in clear, unequivocal terms"; the open community places a premium on honesty and affirms "that truth is the obligation we must assume when we are empowered with the use of words" (Boyer, 1990, pp. 8, 9).

The college or university is also a disciplined community, which governs behavior with clear and concise standards that foster the common good. The disciplined community refuses to look the other way or conjure up a "boys will be boys" attitude in the face of antisocial behavior. This sort of community will pursue the health and welfare of each of its members and will refuse to remain silent about sexism, racism, homophobia, and other forms of prejudice and discrimination. It will also deal with issues of chemical and alcohol abuse, sexually transmitted diseases, vandalism, sexual harassment, and other social problems, with a consistent regard for the community's well-being.

Finally, Boyer (1990) looks to the college or university to be a caring community. This necessitates that students and others be treated as individuals, persons of intrinsic worth, rather than as cogs in the campus machine. To be a caring community means to value relationships and encourage the development of intimate subcommunities. It also refers to the pursuit of service to others as a sign of responsible membership in the community.

Application of the Model

The value in this model lies in its ability to teach us about the origins of our moral problems. Returning now to the ethical and political dilemma raised earlier in this chapter, how does this model apply?

Hiring Dilemmas. In the first example, where you must decide between a candidate who has more experience but is less enthusiastic and a candidate who has less experience but more enthusiasm, how does the model apply? Assuming that you have fulfilled your ethical obligations within the skills quadrant (you have screened and interviewed the candidates in an efficient and effective manner, within existing institutional policies), there is no ethical dilemma because there is no conflict between the skills quadrant and other quadrants. It is a tough decision, but not a decision with ethical implications.

However, in that same example, when the affirmative action issue is introduced, the model does apply. In this instance, deciding whom to hire may involve management (What are the affirmative action policies of my institution, and how do they apply in this situation?), individual virtues (What is my personal commitment to affirmative action, and how does it fit with my commitment to hire the most qualified person, regardless of race?), and community values (What course of action results in justice?).

Personal and Institutional Values. This case used the example of debating the institution's policy on South African investments. Assuming that you have skillfully argued your case (satisfied the ethical requirements of the skills quadrant), there may be other quadrants to consider. Obviously, your commitment to the mission and policies of your institution (institutional obligations) must be taken into account but may be in conflict with individual values, in which personal commitment to justice and equality in South Africa resides.

Confidentiality and the Common Good. The third example, in which the privacy and welfare of a rape victim must be weighed against the general welfare and safety of all students, involves two quadrants in the model. Your responsibility (institutional obligations) to uphold the institution's rape policy, which protects the confidentiality of the individual, is clear. But you also have a responsibility (community values) to promote a disciplined community, in which individuals accept their obligations to the group and where well-defined procedures guide behavior for the common good.

Conflicting Interests. The fourth example, in which the tuition freeze may adversely affect your staff but benefit students, involves several quadrants in the model. Your responsibility, with respect to institutional obligations, to support the tuition freeze is certainly relevant. But there is also trouble within the quadrant of community values, because the values of a just and caring community cannot be applied to students (if the tuition freeze is lifted) or to staff (if the tuition freeze is sustained.)

It should be obvious from our discussion of these examples that this model does not provide answers. Rather, as suggested earlier, it provides a way in which administrators may identify the ethical dilemmas of the situations they face and understand the origins of the choices before them.

Final Considerations

While it is true that no ethical problem can be solved before it is identified, it is also true that no model of decision making can relieve an individual from having to make some choices. There is no such thing in life as morally neutral ground. Perhaps the only thing worse than having to make a difficult decision is having to face the consequences of a problem that has festered because it was not dealt with decisively from the start. Some of the most terrible epochs in world history arose not so much because a few individuals were wicked but because most people, generally good people, remained silent when presented with a moral challenge. These sound like cosmic proportions for student affairs professionals, but the point is that choices must be made in all facets of life.

As administrators in higher education, the circumstances that impinge on our moral choices often prevent us from operating in the realm of the ideal. Seldom do we have the luxury of making a perfect moral choice. The clash of values and the conflict of loyalties that make up the professional life of the administrator inevitably lead us to compromise. While we should never become comfortable with compromise, it must be seen as the result of our inability to conform to, and to bring the world into conformity with, our own highest ideals. Thus the question is rarely whether we compromise but when we do. Astute politicians know that not every battle is worth fighting. In such instances, compromise is not evil. Rather, the moral quandary we face involves compromising too soon and on the wrong issues. The astute politician needs to be mindful of the ethical implications of his or her decisions. At the same time, the responsible moral agent must avoid becoming paralyzed by the multiple moral considerations that are part of every political and administrative act. When the student services administrator has learned to operate in such a way so as to allow the political and moral to inform each other, his or her leadership career in higher education has begun.

References

American College Personnel Association. "Statement of Ethical Principles and Standards." *Journal of College Student Development,* 1990, *31,* 197–202.
Aristotle. *The Nicomachean Ethics.* (J.A.K. Thomson, trans.). New York: Penguin, 1977. (Original date unknown.)
Beauchamp, T. L., and Childress, J. F. *Principles of Biomedical Ethics.* (3rd ed.) New York: Oxford University Press, 1989.
Boyer, E. L. "In Search of Community." Speech presented at meeting of the American Council on Education, Washington, D.C., January 1990.
Browne, R.E.C. "Cardinal Virtues." In J. Macquarrie (ed.), *Dictionary of Christian Ethics.* Philadelphia: Westminster Press, 1967.
Canon, H. J., and Brown, R. D. (eds.). *Applied Ethics in Student Services.* New Directions for Student Services, no. 30. San Francisco: Jossey-Bass, 1985.
Deford, F. "A Gentleman and a Scholar." *Sports Illustrated,* April 1989, pp. 86–90, 94–98, 101.
Hauerwas, S. "Character, Narrative, and Growth in the Christian Life." In C. Brusselmans (ed.), *Toward Moral and Religious Maturity.* Morristown, N.J: Silver Burdett, 1980.
Kitchener, K. S. "Intuition, Critical Evaluation and Ethical Principles: The Foundation for Ethical Decisions in Counseling Psychology." *Counseling Psychologist,* 1984, *12,* 43–55.
Kitchener, K. S. "Ethical Principles and Ethical Decisions in Student Affairs." In H. J. Canon and R. D. Brown (eds.), *Applied Ethics in Student Services.* New Directions for Student Services, no. 30. San Francisco: Jossey-Bass, 1985.
Niebuhr, H. R. *The Responsible Self: An Essay in Christian Moral Philosophy.* New York: Harper & Row, 1963.
Ramsey, P. *The Patient as Person: Explorations in Medical Ethics.* New Haven, Conn.: Yale University Press, 1970.
Rest, J. R. "Moral Development in Young Adults." In R. A. Mines and K. S. Kitchener (eds.), *Socio-Cognitive Development in Young Adults.* New York: Praeger, 1986.

M. Lee Upcraft is assistant vice-president for counseling services and program assessment, affiliate associate professor in the College of Education, and affiliate of the Center for the Study of Higher Education at The Pennsylvania State University.

Thomas G. Poole is director of student activities and religious affairs and an affiliate assistant professor of religious studies at The Pennsylvania State University.

There are specific strategies that chief student affairs officers can employ, which will help them position themselves to respond to political and leadership opportunities and deal constructively with their political environments.

Ideas for the Chief

Paul L. Moore

The authors of earlier chapters have provided a wealth of ideas pertinent to the understanding of the political dimension of managing student affairs and how to operate successfully from a variety of perspectives and organizational levels. Their insights are instructive for professionals, whatever their ages and experience. The task in this chapter is to address the world and needs of the chief student affairs officer by capturing a number of the stimulating ideas presented in earlier chapters and combining them with others rooted in experience (mine and that of others) in a concise and, I hope, thought-provoking way. Clearly, there are no textbook solutions to the wonderfully varied, sometimes messy, and frequently tough situations that routinely occur in organizational life. The most we can do is to explicitly identify ideas and perspectives that will stimulate practitioners to think differently about their challenges, relationships, and strategies.

Managing Your Own Business

As is evident in the writing of all the authors of this volume, how you take care of your own business is critical to dealing effectively with the political dimension of student affairs. You will not be an effective political actor if you haven't tended to your own performance and the relationship to your superior.

The Boss. In Chapter Two, Brown illustrated well the importance of the relationship and strategies for dealing with your president. Without a solid relationship with the president, a vice-president is likely to struggle with most aspects of the job. In such instances, maintaining your position may become completely absorbing, leaving little energy and time for managing assigned functions and serving the institution. Without a reasonable relationship, if not the explicit support of the president, every budget discussion, turf battle, or policy debate is potentially debilitating.

The first principle must be to take whatever time and do whatever is necessary to develop and maintain a productive relationship with your boss. Without it, your effectiveness may be seriously diminished, as may that of your division. While you may begrudge the time, at minimum it may give your staff the freedom to do their jobs and serve students, without unwarranted intrusions from senior management.

Your Competence. Appleton, in his discussion of personal power in Chapter One, notes the sometimes underplayed value of sheer competence. As has been echoed throughout the book, being able to perform well and consistently is perhaps the greatest strength that any of us have as we work and sometimes struggle with others to make our institutions better and more responsive.

Positioning Yourself

Developing a sound relationship with your boss and achieving and sustaining a high level of organizational and professional competence set the stage for improving your ability to influence institutional direction and decision making. In order to work effectively in the larger arena—that is, the institution beyond the confines of the student affairs division—you must position yourself to be most effective.

Visibility. Being visible helps establish that you are interested in the activities of the institution and, depending on the situation, that you are an important player. Visibility is not just going to every student or institutional event. Showing support to various groups, persons, and programs is surely necessary and helpful; however, you physically cannot do everything, and too much exposure can make your appearances expected and commonplace. Your public exposure requires management. It is important to explicitly rehearse why going to a particular meeting, reception, or program is important and whether the visit will contribute to that purpose. Furthermore, it is useful to understand what not attending will signal, because that, too, will be interpreted.

Visit your departments frequently, both announced and unannounced. Impromptu visits and an occasional visit to a staff meeting will signal interest, provide impressions of office style and service orientation, and give you access to an enormous amount of informal communication about what is happening in the unit and on campus. To know in a direct way what is going on requires you to put yourself into situations where informal conversations can occur.

Do not limit yourself to contact with your staff. Get to know people in offices across the institution. People often care less about where they report than who appreciates and takes them seriously. Be consistently and thoughtfully visible.

The Score. Positioning yourself to influence institutional decisions and directions involves ensuring that others understand your abilities and commitments. Keep track of accomplishments, and report them to the president and other important persons and groups. If you do not keep track of your accomplishments, you cannot effectively inform others, and if you do not keep others informed, judgments will be made on the effectiveness of your performance and that of your division, on the basis of what people believe to be true. Your president and campus community need to know what you are doing and how well you are doing it.

Keeping track of your accomplishments also helps you understand whether you are doing what you set out to do, particularly over the longer haul. Individual accomplishments, particularly the smaller and usual victories of staff, need a context for their importance and contributions to be measured and understood. Seeing the broad range of contributions from several units provides context and meaning to individual actions and confirms progress toward larger goals. The vice-president may have the only platform from which to effectively communicate staff achievements.

Look for some easy victories. Too often, we tackle exclusively the big and important but somewhat intractable problems, which may need years rather than months for solution. You and your staff need periodic victories to maintain visibility and the confidence of others and yourselves.

Your Public Presence. Personal style is related not only to how we manage others but also to how others perceive us. "Personal style is the professional demeanor by which each of us is known. It denotes how we behave in our work, as distinguished from what we do" (Appleton, Briggs, and Rhatigan 1978, p. 139). How you are perceived will affect what you can get done and whom you can influence. While many aspects of our styles may be rooted in our backgrounds, our physical attributes, and the like, all elements of style can be understood and assessed for their impact on others. Do you talk the language of those you would influence, or do you use student affairs jargon? Are you a willing and effective speaker, or do you shy away from these sometimes onerous but important tasks of leadership? Do your office style and dress reflect the expectations of students, your peers, and the off-campus visitors you receive from time to time? In short, do you look, act, and see yourself as a key decision maker and particpant in the affairs of your institution?

Informing Yourself. Know your business. While it is obviously impossible to know everthing that is happening within your division, and while too much intrusion on your part is also too confining for your staff, it is critical that you have a good sense of the issues and activities of your departments, particularly in those areas where criticism or turf battles are likely. It can weaken your position, for example, if the administrative vice-president knows more about your financial aid program or auxiliary enterprises than you do. You need to understand the operational details, but it can also be helpful to be acquainted with the information and publications regularly reviewed by other officers. In the case of auxiliaries, receiving the National Association of College and University Business Officers' publications can be enormously helpful in keeping abreast of federal requirements and the thinking of business affairs officers generally.

The vice-president for student affairs is also advised to identify, understand, and follow the major institutional issues, whether or not they directly impinge on student affairs responsibilities. An institutionwide role and the opportunity for broad influence are more likely to come to an officer who is well versed in the full range of institutional concerns.

Know how your institution works. As Bloland has pointed out in Chapter Three, the academic structure has an extensive decision-making and consultative structure, about which student affairs officers ought to be knowledgeable. Whether or not you are a member, you ought to understand in great detail the structure, processes, and rules of the faculty or academic senate. Staff councils, student senates, union organizations, and administrative councils and committees are typical campus organizations with which you should be familiar; for some, trustee and system structures will be important. In addition to the formal structure, an understanding of who makes what decisions with what kinds of advice is local lore of great value. Be a student of the budget process, for substantive educational and organizational issues are frequently explored and decided in this arena.

Smith, in her discussion of small and religious institutions (Chapter Five), has emphasized the importance of knowing the institution's history and culture, which provide a rich store of cues about the institution's ways of doing things, core values, the involvement of various actors in decision making on key institutional issues, and past successes and failures. Knowing the history and the people who were part of it also demonstrates a real interest in the institution, which will help give faculty, staff, and alumni who are committed to the place the confidence that you understand, respect, and will deal carefully with their interests and commitments.

Some of what one needs to know is not available as hard data or in the form of completed reports. It is important, therefore, to develop an awareness of what is happening or communicated around the edges of the organization, outside the formal organization. Earlier in this volume, Brown (Chapter Two) talked about the positive value of gossip, while Mamarchev and Williamson (Chapter Six) urged practitioners to understand both the formal and informal dimensions of colleges and universities. Some veteran administrators talk about pattern recognition—that is, noting seemingly isolated and fragmentary bits of information and ultimately putting them into a mosaic, which helps them understand the actions, motives, and intentions of other political actors. I have kept a dated log of conversations, decisions, rumors, and expectations, to help myself see developing patterns.

The informed and prepared administrator is obviously more likely to be able to take advantage of opportunities presented by timing. Preparation and timing are intimately related. In many situations, timing is the critical variable, determining the success or failure of an initiative or decision, such as when a faculty committee is ready to hear the informed analysis of a problem or a colleague is prepared to deal with a mutual concern. Being prepared makes the opportunties provided by timing more productive.

What You Do When You Are Doing It

This volume is full of ideas and perspectives that the practitioner can apply or at least employ to help work through political situations. Here are several action-oriented suggestions that deserve highlighting.

Relationships. Good relationships with colleagues, staff, faculty, and institutional supporters may be among the most important strategies you can follow. Relationships develop over time and do not just happen. They require nurturing and deliberate action. It is surprising how many people feel awkward initiating relationships. Take the responsibility, and do not demand reciprocity (that is, requiring the second lunch to be initiated by the other person). Develop excuses to talk to people or have lunch. One can even have meetings with no agenda other than the opportunity to check in or see how mutual interests are evolving.

From business meetings can come friendships, which are more durable and dependable, not to mention pleasurable, than the usual work relationships. Of course, good working relationships are mutually obligating. One must be prepared to be a constant colleague or friend if one is to seriously implement this highly personal strategy.

Stressful Relationships. Some relationships do not work and seemingly cannot be turned around. If you cannot ignore them, what do you do? Difficult relationships can test all the human relations skills that you have accumulated over a lifetime of student affairs work. Nevertheless, all of us from time to time experience these often painful and certainly frustrating relationships.

It is sometimes helpful to take a hard look at the people with whom relationships are so difficult. Try to understand their usual tactics and strategies. For example, if their typical tactic is to try to embarrass you or put you on the defensive in a meeting of the president's staff, anticipate those issues and talk about them privately in advance with the president, or have some counterpoints ready. Look also for tendencies and weaknesses, and develop (in your mind, at least) strategies to counter or exploit them. As dysfunctional as such behavior seems, it may be necessary to achieve equilibrium.

Of course, the reverse is also necessary. You should look at yourself, to understand your inclinations and values and determine what causes you to react to the other person the way you do. For example, I have always had a great distaste for interpersonal conflict and typically avoid it at all costs. However, avoidance is not always possible, and some individuals will "push that button," with the result that I have developed postures or strategies that can be tailored to the specific situation, to help me cope.

Whatever coping strategies you employ, do not run from the field of battle, for that has the effect of eliminating you as a competitor. Take the high road, as much as possible. If someone must be negative and destructive, let it be someone else. The campus will ultimately understand the difference of approach. You must, of course, play the game for the long term.

Make sure that your senior staff understand the situation and help with containment. While most of us do not wish to involve our staffs unnecessarily in such matters, you frequently cannot mount a defense against an aggressive or negative colleague by yourself. As we often tell others but fail to observe ourselves, find a personal source of relief, or a perspective that helps you desensitize yourself to what is difficult about the situation. When in doubt, try a little humor.

Strategy for Academic Deans. The deans are frequently at the heart of the academy and will often have significant influence on a wide range of issues. While their influence on student affairs issues may not always be direct, singly or collectively they may have a veto. Moreover, to have their support, particularly on educationally related matters, can be of great assistance.

Further, deans frequently will not have much direct knowledge of student affairs or what you do. Know them. Educate them. Support them, and they will support you. Deliberately seek common projects. The delivery of student services to academic units, particularly in larger institutions, is a perennial issue and one ripe for common action with deans.

As already noted, one need not have specific agenda items to build these relationships. Simply checking in once each semester, to see if there are student or service issues developing that deserve your attention or common action, will be welcomed. Regular lunches also build rapport and a common agenda. A real benefit of regular contact is the development of personal friendships, which are both organizationally productive and personally rewarding.

Dealing with the Media. Too many see the media as unwanted guests at the academy, unwelcome intruders who can only hurt your interests or reputation through misquotes, differing perspectives, and revelations. This perception applies not only to the off-campus print and electronic media but also to our own campus newspapers.

We all have stories to tell about problems of media management and accuracy, but the checks-and-balances function of the news media can be a great ally, in practice as well as in theory. Earlier in this volume, Appleton (Chapter One) described the control of information as being an aspect of bureaucratic power. Most of us have experienced decision-making situations in which the participation of various groups is reduced by the failure to inform them either that a particular issue is to be considered or of the forum in which the decision is to be made. The press, if made aware, can bring to public attention and broaden the discussion of critical issues. All the media may need is some guidance about the general nature of an issue. There are, of course, important ethical and trust issues involved in working with the media on matters of political importance. One must ensure that confidences are not broken and administrative directives not violated.

Another aspect of dealing with the media, one not always appreciated, is the opportunity for communication with a variety of persons and groups that is afforded by being accessible. Nearly every question asked by a reporter gives the opportunity to target the response, regardless of the intent of the reporter. A question about a specific residence hall practice can give the opportunity to speak to faculty about the educational philosophy of the residence hall program, to the president about an administrative detail or policy, and to the student body about how you consider problems that affect them.

Of course, the best way to have the media as a resource is to be accessible (obviously, within institutional policy and restraints). Be a trustworthy and dependable source of information, and have a relationship with the persons who would gather news from you.

Rules of Battle. If you have to fight, how do you do it? There is no administrator with any length of tenure who has not had to fight some other administrator or unit over turf, budget, policy, or something less noble. However distasteful, aggravating, or unnerving, it will occasionally be necessary. Certainly, how one goes about it will reflect personal style, values, and experience. These ideas may be helpful.

Know your stuff. To get caught without critical data or analysis can be deadly. If you are not adequately prepared, postpone the conflict, if you can, until you are. The best strategy, of course, is to anticipate the battle and prepare for it well in advance, even though your first choice is to avoid the conflict completely. To the extent possible, choose when and where you will fight. Your office may have some psychological value for you, and private sessions are usually better than public sessions. If you are prepared and conflict is inevitable, perhaps calling a meeting on the issue will show your confidence and strength.

As Appleton urges in Chapter One, avoid fighting at all, if possible, if winning is not likely. Losing rarely brings benefits to you or your division. Moreover, do not fight if you do not have a clear goal in mind. Fighting for fighting's sake rarely accomplishes anything and is not likely to be seen by others as productive or beneficial to the organization. Perhaps most important, do not fight over trivial matters. Fighting consumes time, drains energy, and, all too often, does not produce long-term organizational or political benefits.

Integrity. When all is said and done, your consistent, ethical behavior will be extremely important to you and your institution. Whatever the stakes and however tough the battles, most people will acknowledge, appreciate, and support leaders with great integrity. Lose it, and you risk losing your constituencies, your boss, and your effectiveness.

Is All This Necessary?

Is all this necessary—all the tactics, strategies, and suspicion? If one looks at how organizations really behave, how the actions of individuals are motivated by a variety of sometimes self-serving motives, and how leaders who would move organizations in new directions are challenged by the human dimension of organizations, one must answer yes. Colleges and universities are political as well as bureaucratic, sometimes rational, human institutions. The argument of this volume is that student affairs administrators must understand the political dimension of colleges and universities if they are to successfully meet the expectations of their institutions, the staffs they lead, and the students and faculty they serve. An understanding of the political dimension of student affairs can best be attained through a frank look at what actually happens in human organizations as various interests compete with one another to influence the decisions and direction of the institution. Next should come a realistic assessment of how one might respond.

The opportunity for dynamic leaders to shape the political environments of our institutions should not be underestimated. Leaders can shape and broadly share the vision that promotes common action. Leaders can model and insist on civil and ethical behavior in the processes that allocate resources, exercise authority, and build policy. Leaders can set the institutional tone that determines how we treat students and each other. Political environments are neutral; those of us who, with our leaders, work in them make them productive and purposeful or negative and painful.

We can take politics too seriously, of course. As a valued colleague observed, "You can be as political as anything, but if you do not act politically for the purpose of helping students and your institution, then it is self-serving and counterproductive." Without high purpose and joy in what we do, our work makes little sense.

In the end, all of us—students, faculty, and staff—will thrive in a college or university community that, in the words of the Carnegie Foundation for the Advancement of Teaching (1990), sees itself as purposeful, open, just, disciplined, caring, and celebrative and ensures that its political processes operate accordingly.

Annotated Bibliography

Bacharach, S. B., and Lawler, E. J. *Power and Politics in Organizations: The Social Psychology of Conflicts, Coalitions, and Bargaining.* San Francisco: Jossey-Bass, 1980.

This book is concerned about intraorganizational relations and brings together the analysis of structure with perspectives on power, bargaining, and coalition building. Its utility is primarily in its development of theory.

Baldridge, J. V. *Power and Conflict in the University.* New York: Wiley, 1971.

An older reference, this work continues to provide some of the best research and analysis of the university as a political organization. It is based on a study of New York University in the late 1960s.

Baldridge, J. V., Curtis, D. V., Ecker, G., and Riley, G. L. *Policy Making and Effective Leadership.* San Francisco: Jossey-Bass, 1978.

This is a comparative analysis of decision making and governance in colleges and universities utilizing the political model. Of particular interest is Chapter 2, which updates the political model outlined in Baldridge's earlier work.

Barr, M. J. "Managing Important Others." In M. L. Upcraft and M. J. Barr (eds.), *Managing Student Affairs Effectively.* New Directions for Student Services, no. 41. San Francisco: Jossey-Bass, 1988.

This chapter contains a number of excellent suggestions for working with constituencies, from students through governing boards.

Bennis, W., and Nanus, B. *Leaders: The Strategies for Taking Charge.* New York: Harper & Row, 1985.

This volume is a statement about leadership, derived from interviews of successful leaders and set in the context of current leadership theory.

Bolman, L. G., and Deal, T. E. *Modern Approaches to Understanding and Managing Organizations.* San Francisco: Jossey-Bass, 1984.

The authors present an excellent discussion of the structural, human resources, symbolic, and political approaches to understanding organizations. For those interested in the political perspective, Chapters 8 and 9 are particularly helpful.

Carpenter, D. S., Paterson, B. G., Kibler, W. L., and Paterson, J. W. "What Price Faculty Involvement? The Case of the Research University." *NASPA Journal*, 1990, 27 (3), 206–212.

This is a very good view of faculty values and concerns in a research university, with ideas for facilitating faculty's involvement in student affairs.

Fisher, J. L. *The Power of the Presidency.* New York: Macmillan, 1983.
This primer on the college or university presidency, while not written from a political perspective, does identify issues and strategies useful in managing the political dimension of the campus. It is nicely grounded in current leadership theory and research.

Pfeffer, J. *Power in Organizations.* Marshfield, Mass.: Pitman Publishing, 1981.
This is an excellent reference on power and is written primarily from a sociological point of view. Chapters deal with assessing power, sources of power, the importance of language and symbols, tactics and strategies, and the perpetuation of power.

Tonn, J. C. "Political Behavior in Higher Education Budgeting." *Journal of Higher Education,* 1978, *49* (6), 575-587.
Tonn sees college and university budgeting as a political process. Included are discussions of political behavior, power bases, strategies for gaining and maintaining power, and elements necessary to gain some congruence between organizational and individual and group objectives in the interest of organizational effectiveness.

References

Appleton, J. R., Briggs, C. M., and Rhatigan, J. J. *Pieces of Eight.* Portland, Ore.: NASPA Institute of Research and Development, 1978.
Carnegie Foundation for the Advancement of Teaching. *Campus Life: In Search of Community.* Princeton, N.J.: Princeton University Press, 1990.

Paul L. Moore is vice-president for student affairs at California State University, Chico.

INDEX

Academic faculty. *See* Faculty, academic
Academic values. *See* Values: academic
Achievements, tracking, 97
Advocacy. *See under* Students
Affirmative action, 82, 91
African American professionals: experiential differences of, 67, 70-72; on managing organizational politics, 68-76
Alliances, building, 49-53, 69, 73, 99, 100
Ambiguity: bureaucratic role of, 46-48; conflict and, 22, 25, 46-48; moral choice and, 86-87, 92-93
American College Personnel Association (ACPA), 83-84, 93
American Council on Education, 37, 41
Appleton, J. R., 6-7, 15, 97, 104
Aristotle, 88, 93
Armstrong, A., 44, 54
Austin, A. E., 46, 54
Autonomy: ethical principle of, 85-86; job, 48-49
Awareness. *See* Visibility of student affairs

Bacharach, S. B., 103
Baldridge, J. V., 1-2, 10, 103
Barker, R. G., 58-59, 64
Barr, M., 38, 41, 103
Beauchamp, T. L., 85, 93
Behavior, individual. *See* Ethics; Values
Bennis, W., 14, 15, 23-24, 26, 103
Bibliography, annotated, 103-104
Biomedical ethics, 85
Black professionals. *See* African American professionals
Block, P., 57, 64
Bolman, L. G., 1, 3, 103
Boss, the. *See* President, the college or university
Boyer, E. L., 59, 64, 88, 90-91, 93
Briggs, C. M., 6-7, 15, 97, 104
Brown, R. D., 83, 84, 93
Browne, R.E.C., 88, 93
Brubacher, J. S., 37, 41
Bureaucratic roles. *See* Roles, bureaucratic

Canon, H. J., 83, 84, 93
Caplow, T., 33, 41
Caring, communal, 77, 87, 91, 92
Carnegie Foundation for the Advancement of Teaching, 102, 104
Carpenter, D. S., 36, 41, 103
Case study (minority professionals), 67-68, 78; eight themes identified by, 68-76; survival strategies, 76-77
Change, effecting. *See* Power, organizational
Chart, organization. *See* Structure, the institutional
Chief student affairs officers: action-oriented strategies of, 38-40, 43, 76-77, 99-102; the boss and the, 23, 53, 95-96; competence of, 18, 77, 96; leadership by, 12-14; learning facilitation by, 19-20; middle managers and, 43-44, 47, 48-49; peer roles of, 24-26; personal style of, 97; positioning of, 76-77, 96-99; power bases of the, 7-9; public presence of, 37-38, 73-74, 97; self-respect by, 18, 74, 97; surrogates for the, 20, 26; as vice-presidents, 20-26; visibility, 21, 39, 62, 96-97
Chief student affairs officers. *See also* Middle managers, student affairs
Childress, J. F., 85, 93
Choice: of battles, 75, 77, 92-93; moral, 92-93. *See also* Decision making, organizational
Coercion. *See under* Power, organizational
Colleges and universities: political environment of, 5-6, 27-28, 90-91, 102; power bases in the, 6-9; religious, 57-59; small and independent, 57-59
Common good, questions of, 82-83
Communication, 58; avenues of social, 72-73; with the faculty, 38-41; filtering, 22-23; informal or gossip, 25-26, 60, 62, 69, 70, 72-73, 96, 98-99; log of, 77, 98-99; of philosophical values, 22, 62; with the president, 22-23
Competence, professional, 7, 9, 37-38, 51-52, 77, 96

ORDERING INFORMATION

NEW DIRECTIONS FOR STUDENT SERVICES is a series of paperback books that offers guidelines and programs for aiding students in their total development—emotional, social, and physical, as well as intellectual. Books in the series are published quarterly in Fall, Winter, Spring, and Summer and are available for purchase by subscription as well as by single copy.

SUBSCRIPTIONS for 1991 cost $45.00 for individuals (a savings of 20 percent over single-copy prices) and $60.00 for institutions, agencies, and libraries. Please do not send institutional checks for personal subscriptions. Standing orders are accepted.

SINGLE COPIES cost $13.95 when payment accompanies order. (California, New Jersey, New York, and Washington, D.C., residents please include appropriate sales tax.) Billed orders will be charged postage and handling.

DISCOUNTS FOR QUANTITY ORDERS are available. Please write to the address below for information.

ALL ORDERS must include either the name of an individual or an official purchase order number. Please submit your order as follows:
Subscriptions: specify series and year subscription is to begin
Single copies: include individual title code (such as SS1)

MAIL ALL ORDERS TO:
Jossey-Bass Inc., Publishers
350 Sansome Street
San Francisco, California 94104

FOR SALES OUTSIDE OF THE UNITED STATES CONTACT:
Maxwell Macmillan International Publishing Group
866 Third Avenue
New York, New York 10022

OTHER TITLES AVAILABLE IN THE
NEW DIRECTIONS FOR STUDENT SERVICES SERIES
Margaret J. Barr, Editor-in-Chief
M. Lee Upcraft, Associate Editor